THE COMPLETE START-TO-FINISH
MBA
ADMISSIONS GUIDE

By Jeremy Shinewald of **mba**Mission

Manhattan Prep Publishing • New York

The Complete Start-to-Finish MBA Admissions Guide

Published by Manhattan Prep Publishing, Inc.
138 W 25th St, 7th Floor
New York, NY 10001
www.manhattanprep.com/publishing

ISBN-10: 1-937707-37-7
ISBN-13: 978-1-937707-37-8
eISBN: 978-1-937707-38-5

20 19 18 17 16 15 14

Layout Design by Dan McNaney and Cathy Huang
Cover Design by Dan McNaney
Cover Photography by Ashly Covington

To Samantha, Imminent, Moishe and Boulder

COMPLETE START-TO-FINISH GUIDE

Jeremy Shinewald

About the Author

Often quoted in major media outlets (including the *Wall Street Journal, U.S. News & World Report* and *Bloomberg Businessweek*) on MBA admissions–related matters, Jeremy Shinewald is the founder and president of mbaMission, the world's leading business school admissions consulting firm. mbaMission is the only MBA consulting firm recommended by Manhattan Prep and Kaplan GMAT, the two largest GMAT test prep providers in the world. Shinewald is a highly sought after speaker on business school admissions topics, addressing audiences in New York, Dubai, London, Tel Aviv, Los Angeles and other major cities on a regular basis.

Before founding mbaMission, Shinewald was chief speechwriter for the Ambassador of Israel to the United States, for whom he wrote more than 70 speeches. He was admitted to several top domestic and international MBA programs himself and ultimately became one of the youngest members of his class at the University of Virginia's Darden School of Business, where he was an admissions interviewer, wrote a business ethics case and was chosen by his peers to be Class Graduation Speaker.

Shinewald is a founding member of the Board of Directors of the Association of International Graduate Admissions Consultants, an organization committed to upholding the highest standards of ethical practice in MBA advisory services. He is also a founding board member of Venture for America, a nonprofit organization committed to providing talented undergraduates with positions in the "trenches" at start-ups.

TABLE OF CONTENTS

INTRODUCTION

INTRODUCTION

"I didn't know what I wanted to do after college, so I applied to the business schools at Harvard and Stanford. I think all I needed to do was send a transcript and fill out a basic form. I got accepted at Harvard, but Stanford asked me to get a year of work experience first, so I decided to go to HBS. Getting in just wasn't that big a deal."

If it were only so easy… The words above were spoken by a member of Harvard Business School's (HBS's) Class of 1968, and what is undoubtedly clear to you is that times have certainly changed. These days, HBS receives approximately 9,000 applications each year for the 900 available seats in its next incoming class. Meanwhile, Stanford gets more than 6,000 applications for its roughly 400 spots. Obviously, getting into a top MBA program now requires more than sending in a transcript and sitting back and waiting for an acceptance letter. In fact, the business school application scene has become so competitive that this graduate—and countless others—laments, "I never would have gotten in today."

Competition for a place in the leading business schools' student body is intense and truly global. Every year, admissions officers shake their heads in wonder at the amazing candidates they simply do not have room to accept. Even if you have a competitive profile, many other highly qualified candidates want that place, too—and will battle you for it. In the end, whether you succeed or fail depends on how you communicate with your target school's admissions committee. And with competition this fierce, you cannot expect to be able to write a standout application in a single afternoon.

We have written this book—and included numerous exercises and examples—to guide you in using your time wisely and effectively to make the most of the application process. After more than a decade of helping MBA applicants get into the top American and international business schools, we know what it takes to compel an admissions committee to send that coveted letter of acceptance. That is not to say that we possess special admissions "secrets" or "shortcuts," however—those simply do not exist. A successful application requires time and *work*, and this book will help ensure that your efforts are targeted and productive.

In this book, we give you the tools to identify and tell your unique stories so that your best qualities shine through in your applications. We will show you how to brainstorm effectively, draft outlines for your essays, make personal statements truly personal, tailor your résumé to the admissions committee's needs, approach your recommenders strategically, prepare extensively for your interviews and much more.

Although the business school application process can certainly be stressful, it definitely does not need to be. With some basic organization and a straightforward strategy, completing your application can actually be enjoyable and rewarding!

We encourage you to visit our Web site, www.mbamission.com, where we offer complete and detailed analysis of the essay questions for the top American and international business schools, as well as free weekly writing tips, lesser-known facts about the leading MBA programs and exclusive interviews with these schools' admissions directors. Explore our blog and return to it frequently—we are constantly updating it and adding new, free resources.

Of course, the information in this guide and the analysis and tips on our site are no substitute for working with a dedicated mbaMission professional. Each MBA candidate is unique. We all have distinct personal stories to tell, and we all face challenges in telling them. mbaMission consultants are specifically trained to help you share your experiences in the most interesting and compelling way possible and to guide you in taking advantage of every opportunity along the way that might help you gain admission to your ideal MBA program.

We hope you enjoy and benefit from this book. If you need additional advice on any element of applying to business school, please feel free to contact us for a free consultation.

Jeremy Shinewald
info@mbamission.com
www.mbamission.com
646-485-8844

CHAPTER 1

FUNDAMENTALS OF AN MBA CANDIDACY

FUNDAMENTALS OF AN MBA CANDIDACY

As you contemplate the strength of your MBA candidacy, several questions will no doubt arise: "Are my grades good enough? What is a strong GMAT score? How much work experience do I need?" Before you begin working on your applications, you first need to understand the components of your profile. By considering these questions well in advance of your application year, you will be able to outline the steps you must take to become a competitive candidate, reduce your potential for disappointment and simplify the task of applying to business school. In this chapter, we will introduce you to the core aspects of your profile that the admissions committees will be evaluating:

- Your Statistics — GMAT/GRE Score and GPA
- Your Professional Experience
- Your Community Profile
- Your Personal Profile
- Your Fit with Your Target Programs

Thereafter, we briefly touch on the components of a business school application:

- Your Scores, GPA and Transcript
- Your Résumé
- Your Essays
- Your Interview
- Your Recommendations
- Your Short-Answer Responses

YOUR MBA PROFILE

YOUR STATISTICS

The GMAT

Here is a simple truth about business schools: they are *all* quantitatively rigorous. Myths abound about one school or another being a "quant school," but anyone who has gone to business school will tell you that earning an MBA is a highly analytically and quantitatively driven academic experience, period. So, when admissions committees examine your "numbers," they are first and foremost asking, "Will this candidate be able to handle our academic program?"

Your GMAT score(s) and grades reveal your "intellectual horsepower," with your GMAT score(s) holding more sway in general—though assigning a specific weight to one metric or another is impossible. We must note that no particular set or level of scores will guarantee that you will get into a top school. Some MBA programs even brag about the number of candidates with 780 scores they reject each year (780 is considered a whopping GMAT score—the highest possible score is 800). Meanwhile, most leading business programs will accept a few applicants with scores that dip into the mid or high 500s (see Table 1), because other components of these applicants' profiles are so strong that the candidates' low GMAT scores can be viewed as aberrations. So, there is no hard and fast rule about what score is "good enough" for any given program or candidate, but a good way to get a sense of your competitiveness is by consulting the average/median GMAT scores and ranges for students at your target schools.

Table 1. GMAT Scores and Ranges at Top MBA Programs, Class of 2015

	Average GMAT	Median GMAT	GMAT % Range[1]	GMAT Range High	GMAT Range Low
Harvard Business School	n/a	730	100%	780	550
Stanford Graduate School of Business	732	n/a	100%	790	550
Wharton	725	n/a	100%	790	630
Columbia	716	n/a	80%	760	680
Chicago Booth	723	n/a	n/a	n/a	n/a
MIT Sloan	713	n/a	80%	760	670
Kellogg	715	n/a	n/a	n/a	n/a
Yale	714	n/a	80%	740	690
Tuck	718	n/a	100%	780	530
Michigan Ross	704	n/a	80%	750	650
Darden	706	n/a	n/a	n/a	n/a
Duke Fuqua[2]	n/a	n/a	80%	740	640
NYU Stern	721	n/a	80%	760	680
UC Berkeley Haas	714	n/a	80%	750	680
Cornell	n/a	700	n/a	n/a	n/a
UCLA Anderson	707	n/a	80%	750	660

[1] *Denotes the percentage of students included in the calculation of the school's GMAT range (e.g., 80% excludes the highest and lowest 10%; 50% excludes the highest and lowest 25%).*
[2] *Fuqua had released no official figures for the Class of 2015 by the publication of this guide but offered statistics on its site that represent "a typical class."*

For reference, the average GMAT score at schools that are generally considered the top 16 programs (according to various popular rankings) is approximately 716 (though the GMAT is scored in 10s). Anything 700 or above is generally considered a "safe" score, meaning that it would be sufficient for any leading school.

··

ADMISSIONS MYTHS DESTROYED:
I MUST SCORE A 750!

At mbaMission, we frequently hear variations on this question: "Do I need a 750 to get into a top MBA program?" Although a score of 750 on the GMAT can only help, it is definitely not a prerequisite. We wanted to dispel this myth and put some who believe it at ease. Here are a few simple reasons this is just not the case…

1. The Average Is Lower: Average GMAT scores at the top 15 MBA programs range from approximately 700 to 730. Clearly, if the high end of the GMAT average range is 730, the schools cannot expect applicants to have a 750. That would mean that every applicant would be above average, and that just is not possible. Still, if a candidate's score falls below the average, this generally places a greater burden on the other components of the individual's application—so, for example, maybe his/her work experience would need to be stronger than others', or maybe his/her extracurriculars would need to stand out even more. Or maybe we are straying from our main point! The bottom line is that mathematically speaking, many people have a GMAT score below 750.

2. Dee Leopold Says So: mbaMission spoke recently with Dee Leopold (May 2014), the managing director of MBA admissions and financial aid at Harvard Business School, who told us point blank that she assesses each individual differently and neither expects nor demands a target GMAT score. The school just happens to attract a large number of great applicants with high scores, and thus its average remains high. Dee said that she would closely examine a journalist's Quant score and pay

particular attention to an engineer's Verbal score, for example. She is concerned that people obsess over target GMAT scores and specifically said that she will not provide candidates with GRE guidance because she does not want to trigger similar anxieties with regard to that exam as well. She grudgingly acknowledged that no matter how many public declarations she makes to the contrary, applicants simply refuse to believe that she does not have a target—and then insisted again that she does not!

3. Too Few Applicants Have a 750 or Higher: The top 15 MBA programs accept approximately 7,000 candidates each application season. Only approximately 3,700–4,600 GMAT test takers earn scores of 750 or higher each year (depending on whether GMAC counts tests taken or individual test takers), and some are earned by people who do not ultimately apply to business school at all, do not apply to any of the leading schools, take the test only to become a GMAT instructor, pursue an EMBA or part-time MBA instead, are rejected because other aspects of their profile render them uncompetitive... and the list goes on. Basically, the top 15 MBA programs do not receive applications from enough applicants with 750s to entirely populate their incoming class, as evidenced by the schools' mid-80% GMAT ranges, which are typically 650–750.

4. All Schools Take the GRE!: Applicants do not really even need to take the GMAT anymore. Of course, if you do take the GMAT, you should strive to achieve the highest score possible, but if the GMAT is not even required, you obviously would not need to score a 750 to be accepted. (Note: London Business School is the sole "GMAT only" holdout among highly regarded MBA programs; although the GMAT is "preferred"

at Dartmouth Tuck and UCLA Anderson, these schools do accept the GRE.)

We want to be unequivocal: 750 is a great GMAT score, and anyone with such a score should be delighted. However, if you do not fare so well on the exam, you should remain quite hopeful and maintain a positive mind-set, keeping in mind that the admissions process is holistic and encompasses far more than this single metric.

• •

A myth persists that competitive applicants must achieve an 80th percentile score on both sections of the GMAT: Quant and Verbal. As we explain in the next "Admissions Myths Destroyed" later in this chapter, this may have been true years ago, but it is no longer true today. In fact, percentiles are not an ideal way of comparing applicants, because these metrics have "spread" so much over time. Currently, only two scores, a 50 or 51 out of 51, even allow an applicant to claim to be in the 80th percentile or higher on the Quant portion of the test. At mbaMission, we now look to raw scores instead and regard a 46, 47 or higher as indicating a strong quantitative performance, though we also recognize that applicants must understand their abilities within the additional context of their GPAs or other certifications (as we explain later in this chapter in the section on GPAs). With respect to a candidate's Verbal score, we see far less "clustering" of scores near the top and consider a 35, 36 or higher competitive, though again, this also depends on many different variables.

We feel compelled to note that a 46 or 47 raw Quant score and a 35 or 36 raw Verbal score would prove your academic competencies in either of these areas separately, but when these raw scores are combined, the resulting aggregate score would be less than 700. As a result, you would need to perform above this minimum "competency" level to serve the schools' interest in keeping their student GMAT average high for the various rankings. All this said, we emphasize yet again that there is neither a minimum nor a "magic" high score that will get you into your dream MBA program—or keep you out.

Quantitative Score		Verbal Score	
Percentile Ranking	Score	Percentile Ranking	Score
97%	51–60	99%	45–51
88%	50	98%	44
79%	49	96%	42
74%	48	94%	41
68%	47	91%	40
66%	46	89%	39
63%	45	85%	38
Mean Score: 38.03		Mean Score: 27.04	

Source: GMAC, July 1, 2014

Regardless, you should certainly do your best to score above the average at your target school(s), and to that end, we recommend a few ways of ensuring you attain the highest GMAT score possible for you:

- *Study*: This advice may seem obvious, but many candidates do not fully understand that the GMAT is not a test you can simply take "cold." In fact, our friends at Manhattan Prep and Kaplan GMAT inform us that to truly be well prepared for the exam, candidates should dedicate a minimum of 12–13 weeks to study—nine weeks in the classroom and three to four weeks of self-guided study thereafter.

- *Take the test sooner rather than later*: Many candidates do not realize that they can take the GMAT up to five years before submitting their application. Admissions offices generally prefer test scores achieved within the previous four years, but our point is that you do not have to take the test only during the year in which you apply. Further, by taking the test earlier, you leave yourself sufficient time to retake it if you do not score as well as you had hoped (though you can take the test only once per month). Also, by taking the GMAT early, you will free up time closer to the submission deadline to dedicate to other parts of your application.

- *Take the test more than once:* You may be surprised to know that admissions committees actually encourage candidates to take the GMAT multiple times—they want you to do your best, because they consider only your highest test score when calculating their class average, and this average is later used in the all-important MBA rankings. By retaking the test and achieving a higher score, you might help improve your target school's average and thus help boost its position in the surveys. If your GMAT score happens to be weak (i.e., is outside the school's published range), taking the test again is crucial. If you take the test once, score a 590 and then give up, your target school will not be impressed. Even if your score does not ultimately improve the second or even third time, your perseverance will reflect positively on you in the admissions committee's eyes. Although it may seem para-doxical, two 590s are better than one.

Your GMAT score is especially important if you graduated from college more than five years ago, if you have no quantitative academic or profes-sional background or if your undergraduate GPA was below the average for students at your target school(s)—a high GMAT score can sometimes help offset a low GPA. That written, we must stress again that your GMAT score is not everything. Be careful not to invest too much time studying and studying, only to raise your score by ten points. If you have taken the GMAT three or four times and your score has not notably improved, the test is probably telling you something, and you would likely be better served directing your efforts to other elements of your application instead.

• •

ADMISSIONS MYTHS DESTROYED: YOU *NEED* AN 80TH PERCENTILE SCORE TO GET IN!

More and more MBA applicants feel they "need" to score in the 80th percentile on both sections of the GMAT exam (particularly the Quant side) to get accepted to their target program(s), but this is simply not true. Here are several reasons why:

1. The Admissions Officers Say No!: Those pesky admissions officers are constantly trying to get in the way of admissions myths. The following is an excerpt from an mbaMission interview with the assistant dean of admissions at allegedly "GMAT-focused" Columbia Business School.

mbaMission: In the admissions mythology, there is this sense that a "safe" GMAT score is a 700 total score with an 80th percentile on both sides of the test [Quant and Verbal], but Quant scores in particular have really been going up, meaning the percentile for some previously high scores has dropped. So these days, even a 48 out of a 51, for example, will not be an 80th percentile Quant score. Should candidates be worried about the percentiles, or are you looking at their Quant scores in absolute terms?

Amanda Carlson: I know exactly what you're saying, and what I can tell you is a resounding, emphatic "No."… People do not have to have this 80/80 type of a breakdown to be admitted. I can't be emphatic about that enough.

You might say to yourself, "Yes, but that is just *one* admissions officer." Touché! So let us share what Bruce DelMonico, the straight-shooting assistant dean and director of admissions at the Yale School of Management, told mbaMission in an email exchange:

"We don't need to see the proverbial 80/80 split ... . We don't have any cut-offs or thresholds, but we do tell candidates that if they can get to the 60th percentile or above, that will serve them well. Again, we certainly have taken people whose percentiles are lower, but ideally you'd want to be at or above 60%."

And when mbaMission spoke with Dee Leopold, the managing director of MBA admissions and financial aid at Harvard Business School, she was explicit about how the school assesses each candidate on his/her individual merits, rather than on a target GMAT score, which is a natural lead-in to our second rationale…

2. An 80th Quant Percentile Is Not What It Seems: These days, a 49 out of 51 will not get you an 80th percentile score— a 49 is a 79th percentile score. So you need to have either a perfect 51/51 or a 50/51 to even score in the 80th percentile or higher. As Manhattan Prep instructor Ron Purewal noted to us at mbaMission, "The meaning of the Quant percentiles has fundamentally changed. The percentiles just reflect the changing demographics of the GMAT pool." Indeed, the pool has been profoundly affected by an influx of international applicants who earn high scores on the Quant section, but many never apply to top schools in the United States. As a result, the overall Quant scores are rising, and the percentiles are falling, obscuring what the admissions officers at the top 15 schools actually see in their applicant pool. Ron continued, "It's obviously not true that the majority of people walking around at top b-schools are all sporting 50s or 51s on the Quant section."

3. Your Score Is Predictive, Not Your Percentile: The reason we want to destroy this myth is that percentiles have shifted over time, which has created confusion. Raw scores, on the other hand, do not shift and are a far better predictor of performance. A 47 Quant score today represents exactly what a 47 Quant score represented years ago, because the score is standardized. The admissions officers can go through data and correlate student performance with scores, so they should be able to predict whether an individual with a 47 Quant score will flunk out or hit a home run. This is not true of a percentile that fluctuates up and down.

4. The GMAT Is Not the Sole Measure of Competency: The GMAT is only one piece of the puzzle with respect to measuring a candidate's aptitude. Let us say that you were evaluating an individual who had a 3.6 GPA in business administration, had completed Level I of the Chartered Financial Analyst (CFA) and had earned a 47 raw Quant score (68th percentile) on the GMAT. Would you place a bet that this person could manage MBA-level finance, accounting, economics and quantitative methods courses? His CFA Level I achievement alone says that he can, as does his GPA! His GMAT Quant score is actually not all that relevant for assessing his quantitative abilities, because that box has already been checked via his other accomplishments/stats. Now let us say that you were evaluating a 3.8 English/economics double major with a 33 raw Verbal score (69th percentile). Would you feel comfortable allowing her into your class, confident that she could quickly read and digest information? I imagine you would be. A person's GMAT score, GPA and other designations work together to inform the admissions officers—not just that applicant's GMAT percentile(s)!

What is dangerous about the fixation on percentiles is that it is driving candidates to misplace their priorities. Ron Purewal noted that he sees many applicants with scores of 48 or 49 who spend time trying to lift their scores to 50. This is worrying to us, not only because we want people with scores of 48 and higher dedicating time to other parts of their profiles and applications instead, but also because we are concerned that some applicants with a score of 48 (or lower) may unnecessarily become disheartened and decide not to apply. Let us be very clear, high scores and high percentiles are great, but applicants need to look past superficialities and statistics to understand the bigger picture, in context.

• •

Let us end this section on the GMAT with a note on the now not so "new" portion of the exam. In June 2012, the Graduate Management Admission Council (GMAC)—the body that administers the GMAT—added a new section to the test called Integrated Reasoning (IR), which requires that candidates use data sets to make judgments (this a pretty gross oversimplification, but explaining the GMAT in detail is beyond the scope of this book). The IR section of the GMAT is still going through a process of calibration, meaning that admissions officers are waiting to see how people perform on this kind of task in business school before they can correlate the success of the student and the success of the IR test taker. All of this is to say that as of the printing of this book, the verdict on the importance of the IR section in the schools' evaluation process is not yet clear. Most admissions officers are still unsure what to make of the section—and many have admitted this directly to us. So, as of August 2015, you should not be too concerned about your performance on the IR section, though you should of course still do your best. You never know when it will become important.

The GRE

You may be wondering, "All of this emphasis is put on the GMAT, but what about the GRE? Aren't schools interested in the GRE these days?" Yes, most top business schools do indeed accept the GRE, and the test is on even footing with the GMAT at virtually all schools. After all, why would admissions committees offer the option of taking the GRE only to disenfranchise those applicants who then take it? In fact, many of the schools that have begun accepting the GRE have stated that they do so because they are trying to broaden their applicant pool.

The following is an excerpt from an mbaMission interview with MIT Sloan's senior director of admissions, Rod Garcia, that addresses the issue of the "legitimacy" of the GRE in business school admissions:

> *mbaMission*: What can you say about the GRE? Applicants often worry that they are identifying themselves negatively if they take the GRE. Can you dispel that myth?

> *Rod Garcia*: I don't know why people have that perception. Right now, about 5% of our applicants apply with the GRE. So, with a small number of applicants and a test that has changed its scoring, I can't offer a lot of data, but I can tell you that the GRE is definitely not inferior.

Meanwhile, Harvard Business School's managing director of MBA admissions and financial aid, Dierdre "Dee" Leopold, told mbaMission, "We view these tests equally and have no preference."

So, why might you consider taking the GRE rather than the GMAT?

- If you are a cost-conscious applicant, you may appreciate that taking the GRE costs $195, whereas you will need to pay $250 to take the GMAT.

- If you are applying to joint degree programs, these require that you take the GRE—so why study for two tests?

- If you have struggled with the GMAT, particularly the Quantitative section, you may do better on the GRE, because it does not cover the same kind or level of quantitative topics, such as data sufficiency.

The GRE has a reputation for being "easier" than the GMAT, and information provided by Educational Testing Services (ETS), the company that administers the GRE, in fact bears this out. ETS produces a GRE-GMAT comparison tool that reveals, for example, that a 165 GRE Quantitative Reasoning score, which is strong enough for a 90th percentile GRE Quant score, equates to a 47 GMAT Quant score, which is just a 68th percentile GMAT Quant score. What does this say? A strong GRE performance equates to a comparatively weaker GMAT performance—in other words, doing well on the GRE is easier than doing well on the GMAT.

However, before you get too excited about the GRE and think that it is therefore a "better" or "easier" path to business school admittance, remember that admissions officers are not interested in standalone percentiles. Indeed, this is why a 165 GRE Quant score will not get you credit for a 90th percentile GMAT Quant score, but for a 68th percentile score. Admissions officers fully understand how the two tests compare and therefore expect applicants to have higher GRE scores to compensate for the differences in the exams. Further, the schools benchmark current candidates' GRE scores against those of past applicants and can thereby interpret your score relative to that of others who either succeeded or failed in their academic program.

Because admissions officers are far less transparent about GRE scoring, offering you guidance as to what a competitive GRE score would be is rather difficult at this time. We imagine that as the GRE becomes a more popular choice among applicants and as rankings bodies such as *Bloomberg Businessweek* and the *Financial Times* begin demanding information on students' GRE averages, admissions officers will start to become more communicative about their expectations. That said, the popular rankings are not currently considering the GRE in their school evaluations, so this alternate test can present an opportunity for candidates who have proven through their grades that they have the quantitative abilities to manage an MBA program (such as via a 3.9 GPA in mathematics). If such an individual were to find standardized testing a challenge, the GRE might be the better option, because the schools could then accept this candidate knowing that his low GRE score would not affect their standing in any of the rankings. Some regard the GRE as a "back door" to business school for this reason.

The advice we offered with respect to taking the GMAT holds true for the GRE as well:

- *Study:* Preparing for the GRE by taking a GRE study course is strongly recommended over taking the test "cold."

- *Take the test sooner rather than later*: Your GRE score is good for five years, though schools prefer to see results from a test taken within the previous four years.

- *Take the test more than once*: Admissions committees will accept your strongest GRE score, so if at first you do not succeed, try, try again!

YOUR GPA

Admissions committees consider your GPA another important indicator of your ability to succeed in the challenging academic environment that is the MBA classroom. But as with your GMAT/GRE score, there is no "right" number you must have. The average GPA of students at the top MBA programs is approximately 3.5 (see Table 2), but admissions committees also take into account your major, your class ranking (if available), the institution you attended (though to a lesser degree—dozens of schools from around the world are represented in each MBA class) and any trends over time (e.g., did you get all As toward the end of college that offset a few early Cs?). In addition, admissions offices each have their own way of converting scores that do not follow the traditional 4.0 scale.

Table 2. Average GPAs at Top MBA Programs for the Class of 2015

	Average GPA
Harvard Business School	n/a
Stanford GSB	n/a
Wharton	n/a
Columbia	3.5
Chicago Booth	3.57
MIT Sloan	n/a
Kellogg	n/a
Yale	3.57
Tuck	3.5
Michigan Ross	3.4
Darden	3.52
Duke Fuqua	n/a
NYU Stern	3.51
UC Berkeley Haas	3.61
Cornell	3.3*
UCLA Anderson	3.5

Median GPA rather than average.

In particular, admissions officers want to see evidence of your quantitative abilities. If your transcript does not include any management, economics, finance or math classes that prove you have done well in quantitative subjects in the past, you will need to find another way of demonstrating your competencies in these areas. Or, if your GPA is weak in general (less than 3.0), you must find a way to "reposition" yourself as more mature than you were in college and as someone who is now ready to be a dedicated and motivated student. How can you accomplish this? Here are three ways:

1. *Alternate transcript*: You can build a strong "alternate transcript" to submit with your application by taking two or more courses at a local college in subjects that your transcript lacks but that would prove your ability to manage MBA coursework—namely, economics, statistics, calculus, accounting and finance—and by earning As in these classes. These classes would of course need to be completed before you apply to business school, and earning As in the courses is key to reassuring the admissions committees of your capabilities in these areas. Economics, statistics and calculus should command your primary focus, because they are generally considered more rigorous subjects.

2. *Designations*: By passing Level I of the CFA exam—which covers many topics first-year MBA students study—you will reveal that you have the maturity and drive to dedicate yourself to a rigorous self-guided study program and that you have strong pre-MBA knowledge. Note, however, that the CFA program is remarkably time consuming and requires several months of intense study; in addition, the Level I exam is only offered twice a year, and candidates must wait several months to receive results. Thus, we recommend addressing this task well in advance of your targeted MBA application year. Pragmatically speaking, because of the time commitment this exam requires, we only recommend this course of action if the CFA relates directly to your career interests. If it does not, then pursuing the alternate transcript option will

suffice. If you have earned a Chartered Professional Accountant designation, this can also attest to your discipline, maturity and ability to manage MBA course work.

3. *The GMAT*: A strong GMAT Quant score should generally offset a lack of quantitative coursework.

Ironically, your "stats" (your GPA and GMAT/GRE score together) need to be interpreted qualitatively. Although no one would have trouble understanding that an engineer with a 3.8 GPA and a 750 GMAT score could perform well academically in business school and would help boost a school's averages for rankings purposes, most cases are not so cut-and-dried. Can a mathematician with a 3.7 GPA and a 630 GMAT score manage the program, and how would this person's stats affect a school's averages (and in turn, its position in the various rankings)? What about an art history major with a 3.1 GPA and a 730 GMAT score? The admissions offices will carefully examine all the evidence and come to a conclusion as to whether you can manage their program's work and how you might contribute to the school's averages (and rankings). And what might work for one school may not for another. Remember, though, your stats are just one piece of the "holistic" puzzle. What else do admissions committees examine?

YOUR PROFESSIONAL EXPERIENCE

Admissions officers want to be sure that beyond possessing the necessary academic skills, the candidates they admit will be able to participate meaningfully in the MBA classroom and will be successful professionally after they graduate. Your career trajectory and professional accomplishments to date (presented in your résumé, essays, recommendations and interviews) serve as a strong indicator for admissions officers of your classroom and professional potential.

As we have thus far noted about several other elements of an applicant's candidacy, no set rule is in place as to the "right" amount or type of work experience, nor is there a "right" career trajectory. Each year we hear from a few candidates who fear that their professional position is a liability. One day we might hear, "I am a school teacher, and there are so few of us in business school. If only I had gone into consulting or banking, I would have a much easier path into the school of my dreams." Then, the next day we might hear, "I am a consultant. There are so many of us in business school. If only I had chosen a career in education, I would have a much easier path into the school of my dreams." The truth is that no easy path into a top business school exists for any candidate, and although bankers and consultants are certainly well represented in the top MBA programs, this is not evidence of a bias among admissions officers. Instead, this is simply a function of the nature of these workplaces—most bankers and consultants complete two or three years on the job and then need an MBA to progress past a certain point. In contrast, no teacher truly needs an MBA to progress.

Conveying your performance in past endeavors is the best way of demonstrating your potential to the admissions committees. Places are available at all the top business schools for high-performing teachers, consultants and bankers alike—but not for low-performing individuals in *any* field. The leading MBA programs want their students to represent a diversity of experience in their classrooms, and they want candidates who exhibit the promise of achievement—not just a certain job title—going forward.

One thing the admissions committees seek to learn in examining your professional experiences is whether you tend to take on increasing responsibility in your work. This may be evidenced by promotions or by simply having had a notable impact on your department or company through informal influence (without a promotion). After all, the lowest man on the totem pole can have the greatest influence in a project's outcome if he is willing to speak up and get buy-in for his ideas.

Admissions committees are also interested in the kind of impact you have had on others, in either formal or informal ways, such as via direct management, mentorship or training roles. If you have never managed another employee or a team, do not worry. Many candidates applying to business school are in the same position. Leadership and management are actually two different things, and admissions committees take both into account. Whereas management entails directly supervising other employees, leadership can include such broad interpersonal activities as mentorship, training, coaching, influencing and persuading others to adopt your ideas, taking responsibility for an outcome, helping a floundering teammate and creating open and productive communication within a team. More simply, for our purposes, management is the use of *one's position* to gain the best outcomes, and leadership is the use of *persuasion* to gain the best outcomes. Mine your personal and professional history for examples of both, and if examples are lacking, start seeking opportunities now to contribute to others and to take responsibility for the outcome of your work, so you will be able to discuss these in your application. If your job provides an insufficient outlet for leadership, look for opportunities in your extracurricular and community service activities.

At most leading MBA programs, students have an average of approximately five years of work experience (see Table 3), but we remind you that an average derives from a wide range, meaning that some students are above this figure and some below. Every year, candidates with varying degrees of experience are accepted to business school, and having more or less than the average is neither good nor bad. The key factor is what you have been able to accomplish during the years you have worked (whatever the number) and the kind of potential this demonstrates with respect to your post-MBA goals. Admissions committees will look beyond your industry, company name, title and years of experience and focus instead on performance!

Table 3. Average Work Experience at Top MBA Programs for the Class of 2015

	Average Years of Work Experience
Harvard Business School	n/a
Stanford GSB	4
Wharton	5
Columbia	5
Chicago Booth	5
MIT Sloan	5
Kellogg	n/a[1]
Yale	n/a
Tuck	5
Michigan Ross	5
Darden	n/a
Duke Fuqua[2]	5
NYU Stern	4.6
UC Berkeley Haas	5
Cornell	5
UCLA Anderson	5

* Kellogg instead reports a range of 2 to 12.

[2] Fuqua had released no official figures for the Class of 2015 by the publication of this guide but offered statistics on its site that represent "a typical class."

YOUR COMMUNITY PROFILE

In addition to the sincere value that you can bring to your community by volunteering in some way, community work is important for you as an applicant. Contributing to others shows initiative and motivation on your part and can differentiate you from otherwise similar candidates who do not go this extra mile. For example, if you take time outside work to volunteer with the aged while your coworker who is also applying to business school instead uses that time to shop or watch TV, all else being equal, you have an advantage. Simply put, you will have done more and revealed a stronger internal motor. Showing personal commitment to and passion for a cause or organization and seeking leadership opportunities beyond your job indicate that you have strong personal qualities and gives the admissions committee deeper insight into your candidacy.

Still, some applicants mistakenly regard any form of community service as a prerequisite for getting into a top MBA program. These candidates will thus sign up for a volunteer activity without first considering whether it is a reasonable fit for them and/or how their choice could reflect on their candidacy in the admissions committees' eyes. Although community service is a positive, it is not a "one size fits all" element of one's candidacy. As you contemplate your current or potential community involvements, recognize that the number of "hours served" is not as important as the spirit of your participation and the extent of your impact.

We therefore encourage you to carefully consider your community experiences in the same way you would examine and evaluate your professional or entrepreneurial ones. Although people can sometimes make mistakes in their career paths, most gravitate toward areas or opportunities in which they can excel—justifiably to further their own interests. The same is true for volunteer opportunities. If, for example, you have always enjoyed a particularly close relationship with your grandmother and want to share this kind of positive experience with others, you might decide to volunteer to spend time with seniors at a retirement home, where you would naturally be predisposed toward success. If you were quite passionate about your work there, you just might get others involved, expand the retirement home's volunteer program, take greater leadership in the program and more. However, if you are not that passionate about the elderly, but you live near a retirement home, no matter how convenient volunteering there would be, doing so would likely be a mistake for you, because you would lack the spirit of commitment/adventure necessary to ensure that the story of your experience there would be compelling to an admissions committee.

Although accomplishments in the community arena can make great subject matter for essays and clearly illustrate that you seek to make a difference, your charitable involvement does not need to be with a registered nonprofit. For example, you can reveal your altruistic spirit and internal motor through a simple personal commitment to a neighbor, relative or colleague—perhaps by helping this individual with a weekly chore or serving as a social outlet if he or she has few friends in the area. You could also demonstrate your philanthropic nature via a small neighborhood beautification initiative or by organizing fitness classes for colleagues or friends. The key is not the organization involved in your activity but the impact you have as a result; you must show the admissions committees that you aspire to excellence and seek challenges and opportunities for leadership.

If you have not been involved in a community activity up to now, we can reassure you that it is never too late to start. Again, admissions committees are interested in your impact and your altruistic spirit and commitment, rather than total time served. However, the more time you can commit to such an activity, the more opportunity you will have to truly influence and assist others and the more experiences you will be able to discuss in your essays and interviews. So, starting sooner rather than later is certainly beneficial.

Perhaps you have had difficulty committing to any volunteer activities because you work incredibly long hours. The admissions committees know that such situations exist, and they will take this into account when evaluating your candidacy. That said, you can always find *something* to do outside work to show that you are a well-rounded individual and interested in more than just your career. For example, try volunteering at a soup kitchen for a few hours each weekend; look into online volunteering options; spend some vacation time volunteering internationally. Any true effort you devote to a practice or organization outside your office will enhance your profile and give you potentially rich fodder for your essays. We simply recommend finding something in which you are genuinely interested and pursuing that.

YOUR PERSONAL PROFILE

These days, admissions officers unquestionably want to assemble a diverse class. However, diversity should not be misunderstood as being exclusively ethnic, national, religious or related to gender. You can also successfully demonstrate diversity through your community activities, aspects of your professional life or even your personal hobbies and interests. You certainly do not have to worry that you must differentiate yourself in some spectacular way—for example, you do not need to be an Olympic swimmer or to have sold a major start-up to get into business school. If you are helping a sibling through school, writing a blog that has achieved some popularity/notoriety or completing Ironman triathlons, these are largely uncommon personal achievements and can help showcase what makes you unique. In fact, rather than leaving these aspects of your life out of your application, you should try to increase your involvement in them now so you can use them as showpieces. For example, if you have always intended to publish a certain article and have almost finished a final draft, now is the time to finish it. If you have always planned on earning your CFA charter and only have Level III of the exam left to pass, arrange to take the final test this year. If you can run 20 miles and have always dreamed of completing a marathon, do it this year. Do not postpone these projects any longer! We are not suggesting that if you have never run a mile in your life, you start training for a marathon now; however, if a goal of yours is reasonably in sight and will be otherwise achieved after your applications are due, you should accelerate your timeline to ensure that you have completed it before the first-round deadline.

Of course, diversity in the conventional sense is important to highlight as well, if you possess it. For example, if you represent a demographic the schools typically seek, you should certainly showcase this aspect of your profile in your application. Admissions officers want to put together a class that represents a wide range of characteristics across the board. So, whatever kind of diversity you can offer is an important component of your profile as an applicant.

International experience can also be a diversifying factor in your candidacy, and with some schools paying increasingly more attention to this element, many candidates worry that they are lacking in this area. However, an absence of international experience is not an indicator that you will be rejected from a top school any more than having this kind of experience is a guarantee that you will be accepted. Admissions committees understand that not all jobs—or lives—provide opportunities for international experience. If your global exposure is limited at best, consider other ways you can illustrate for the admissions committees a connection with or interest in other countries and cultures, such as learning a foreign language or taking on a work assignment that engages offices outside the United States (even if you never actually leave your desk). The ability to deal with diversity is a key challenge for business leaders and MBA students alike, so the admissions committees want to know that you have encountered and grappled with some of the issues posed by spending time in foreign environments and/or engaging with different people.

YOUR FIT WITH YOUR TARGET PROGRAMS

In addition to assembling a competent, driven and diverse class, admissions officers want to bring together candidates who are a good fit with their school's community and will go out into the world after graduation as positive stewards of the school's brand. In short, in evaluating your candidacy, they want to be sure that _you_ have made the right choice in applying to their school. MBA programs vary vastly from one to the next in a number of areas, including location, class size/structure, curriculum, pedagogy, academic specializations, recruitment focus, alumni base, facilities, rankings and reputation. They also differ culturally and experientially. You should therefore thoroughly research the obvious and subtle differences between programs when choosing the ones you believe are best for you and be ready to discuss the reasons behind your conclusions.

When admissions committees are evaluating your explanation of why you have chosen their school (over others), they will first look for evidence that you truly understand their program—beyond the rankings, taglines, marketing mantras and most popular classes. They want to know that you have extensively investigated the school's culture, spoken with students and/or alumni and really "kicked the tires" of the program to make sure it matches your individual needs and style. If it does not, you represent a risk in that you could accept a place in their class and then be unhappy and/or struggle with the program. So, you must truly do your homework on your target school(s) so that you fully understand why you are applying and what you will gain from your experience there.

COMPONENTS OF AN MBA APPLICATION

Now that we understand the various aspects of your MBA profile—what you need to have in place to begin applying to schools—let us briefly look at the components of the application itself and where the different elements of your profile come into play. In later chapters, we will explore each of these areas in great depth.

- *Your Scores, GPA and Transcript*: Your GPA and GMAT/GRE score(s) are the primary indicators of whether you can handle the rigors and requirements of an MBA program. So, you must have a valid GMAT or GRE score before submitting an application to any school. In addition, you must have earned a degree from a four-year college, though some schools will accept one from a three-year institution if that is the norm in your country. (Note: If you did not attend an English language university, you will have to submit a TEST of English as a Foreign Language [TOEFL] score as well.)

- *Your Résumé*: Virtually all MBA programs will ask you to submit a professional résumé. Keep in mind that your résumé should not serve as just a record of your professional experiences, but also as a summary of your professional, community, academic and personal accomplishments. Because your résumé will touch on virtually all aspects of your profile, it should be crafted very carefully.

- *Your Essays*: For each application you complete, you will need to write two to five essays. These compositions offer an opportunity for you to showcase the various aspects of your candidacy—your professional, community and personal profiles and especially your fit with the MBA program in question. If your statistics represent you well, you will probably not need to discuss your academic accomplishments in your essays, but if you did not perform at a high level in college or on the GMAT/GRE, you can submit an optional essay that explains why the past does not predict the future and that more fully demonstrates your current abilities.

- *Your Interview*: Not every business school applicant will be interviewed, but virtually no candidate is ultimately accepted at a top MBA program without first being interviewed. Like your essays, your interview is an opportunity for you to discuss all aspects of your profile. Interviews are typically 30 minutes in length and are generally only for those candidates who have passed a "cut," rather than being equally open to all applicants.

- *Your Recommendations*: Most schools will ask you for two recommendations, almost always professional ones. In these important documents, your recommenders can discuss your professional successes, personal strengths and sometimes your weaknesses, and can reveal your fit with your target school. No standard recommendation form is used across all schools. Each school poses its own questions and requires its own format, so your recommenders will have their work cut out for them if they provide recommendations for multiple schools on your behalf. Choosing your recommenders carefully is key.

- *Your Short Answer Responses*: Each school's base application form can be incredibly time consuming and typically includes a number of straightforward questions about your family history, education, professional and community service experience and other basic elements of your profile. Many candidates make the mistake of overlooking this portion of the application entirely. Instead, you should carefully and thoughtfully complete these forms—doing so will better allow you to showcase your strengths across the board.

CHAPTER 2

YOUR LONG-TERM PLANNING TIMELINE

Your MBA Application Timeline

The Well-Prepared MBA Applicant

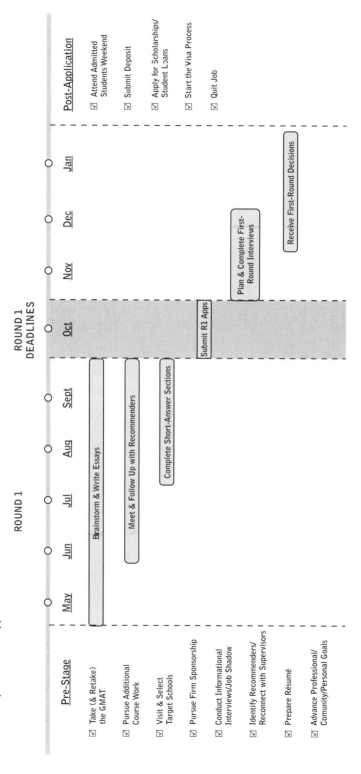

YOUR MBA APPLICATION TIMELINE

The Typical MBA Applicant

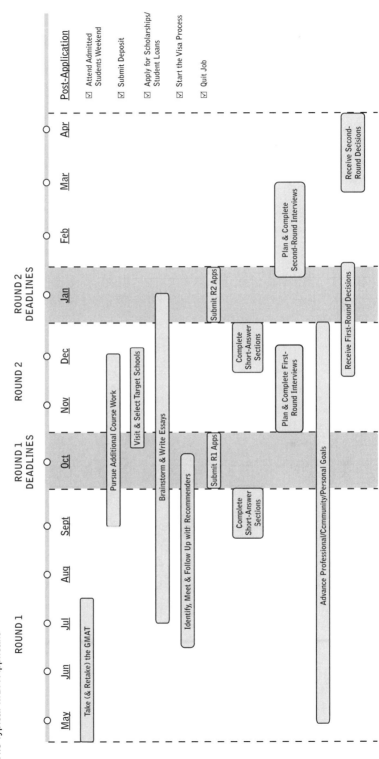

YOUR MBA APPLICATION TIMELINE

The Last-Minute MBA Applicant

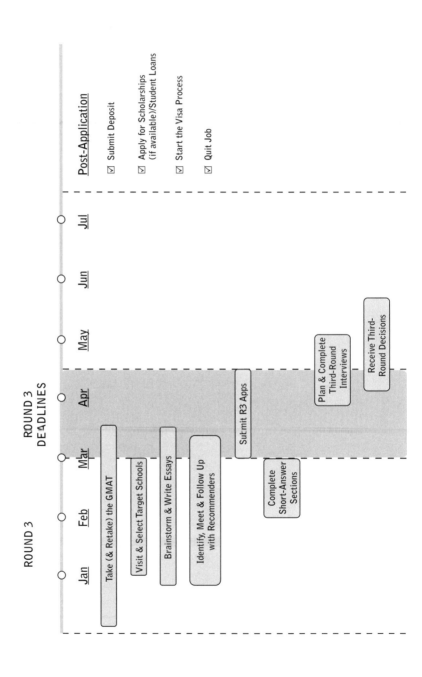

YOUR LONG-TERM PLANNING TIMELINE

In Chapter 1, we outlined the various elements of a business school applicant's profile and a typical application. For a moment, imagine trying to work on maximizing all aspects of your candidacy at once—taking classes while also studying for the GMAT, writing essays, bolstering your professional profile, researching recommenders, committing to community engagements and so on. Trying to manage it all simultaneously would be overwhelming, to say the least! In this chapter, we will guide you through this multifaceted journey by providing a recommended timeline for approaching your pre-application, application and post-application tasks.

Although we offer these practical steps to help you manage the application process, remember that no set "recipe" exists for gaining admission to a top MBA program. No set "to do" list will guarantee your acceptance at a particular school. Your individuality is your greatest asset, and your personal/professional story is crucial in differentiating yourself from other qualified applicants in this ultracompetitive pool. By getting organized now and planning ahead, you will maximize all possible opportunities to enhance your candidacy along the way.

APPLICATION ROUNDS: A PRIMER

Most leading U.S. business schools offer three rounds of admissions, the first in September/October, a second in January and a third in March/April. Here we examine the significance of each round and the signals that applying in each one can send.

<u>Round 1</u>

For years, admissions officers have told candidates that Rounds 1 and 2 are "roughly equivalent" in terms of the competitiveness levels of the applicants in each. These days, "roughly equivalent" typically means "all things being equal, get your application in early or don't bother submitting anything less than your best, even if that means waiting until Round 2." For example, the Tuck School of Business at Dartmouth College tells applicants on its Web site, "It is to your advantage to apply as early as you are ready. The admissions committee cannot predict the quality of future applications, and is therefore inclined to admit well-qualified applicants early in the process… However, it is important not to rush your application." While many schools share Tuck's stance, some take even stronger "pro-Round 1" stands. The Stanford Graduate School of Business, for example, states on its site, "If you are considering applying in either Round 1 or Round 2, we strongly encourage you to consider Round 1."

From an admissions standpoint, applying in Round 1 confers an advantage—at some schools, this advantage is significant, while at others, it is almost imperceptible. Still, if you cannot complete your applications in time to submit them in the first round, you should not assume that the admissions season has passed you by. Most applicants are still admitted in Round 2.

Applying earlier in the season can also be advantageous from a candidate perspective. For example, if you plan to apply to several schools, submitting to one or more programs in the first round will allow you to pace yourself across the first two rounds rather than having all your applications come due at approximately the same time. Moreover, in some cases, you will learn whether you have been admitted to programs to which you applied in the first round before your Round 2 applications are due, and if you are, this could ultimately save you time and energy you would have otherwise spent on completing additional applications. Further, if you are admitted in Round 1 to a program you want to attend, you can spend the winter getting to know the school better, preparing for the program and making summer travel plans. And lastly, in the event you are waitlisted in the first round, the school may reconsider your application in the second (and even third) round, giving you a slightly better overall chance of admission.

In short, Round 1 is the best round for highly organized and motivated applicants. It is also the best round for overrepresented or "flawed" applicants. If you happen to be part of a group that is overrepresented in the applicant pool—male investment bankers or Indian software engineers, for example—submitting your application early would be wise, because your target school will have ample opportunity to fill its class with your demographic. Why wait until the admissions committee has seen and sorted through the majority of your comparable peers? Similarly, if you feel you are a "flawed" candidate—maybe you have a very low GMAT score or GPA but are otherwise quite strong—you should apply early. Schools are only going to accept a small number of applicants with sub-600 GMAT scores, for example. You do not want to be in a position where an admissions officer might think, "Letting in another 580 candidate will damage our GMAT average—a shame, because I love this applicant!"

Round 2

Round 2 is not only when most applicants submit their applications but also the round from which most candidates are accepted. You should not expect that if you apply in Round 2, you will be held to an unreasonably high standard or are applying "too late" to have a fair chance of being accepted.

One thing to keep in mind, though, is that if you start to apply to several schools in the second round, you could find yourself under intense pressure to finish your applications on time and to do them well. Conservative applicants typically apply to five or six MBA programs, and that can be a lot of work to complete between October and January. Doing so is certainly not impossible, but if you are reading this in advance of your expected application year, plan to spread your applications across the first and second rounds—be optimistic that you can get them all done early, but know that you will likely need extra time to do so. From our experience, applicants are rarely able to complete more than four applications in a single round.

- -

ADMISSIONS MYTHS DESTROYED: ROUND 1 IS EVERYTHING

Many MBA admissions officers tell candidates that if they can complete their applications in time to submit them in Round 1, they should do so. Most programs will also tell candidates they should try to avoid Round 3, because most of the available places will have been filled by then. So, what does this say about Round 2?

A strange trend seems to have manifested lately: candidates have been calling mbaMission to ask whether submitting an application in Round 2 is worth the effort or whether the opportunity has passed at that point. Unfortunately, when one is going to be compared against a group of unknown competitors, being concerned about every perceived difference or deficiency is only natural. Some candidates grow concerned if they are a year older than the average student at their target school, while others fret if they are a year younger. Many applicants worry if their GMAT score is ten points below a school's average. And, of course, some worry about submitting their application in Round 2 and how this might affect their chances for admission. However, the overall strength of your candidacy, which is a measure of many factors, is far more important than where you fit in relation to any single statistic—not to mention whether you apply in Round 1 or 2.

So, we too would encourage you to apply early, if you are ready, but we do not believe anyone should give up on their MBA dreams for a year if applying in Round 1 is just not practical. You may be surprised to discover that admissions committees encourage early applications but also concede that the difference in selectivity between the first and the second rounds is very small. To back up this statement, we offer a few quotes from mbaMission's exclusive interviews with admissions officers:

"People ask, generally, is it better to apply in the first round or the second round or third round? We definitely advise people to avoid the third round if possible, because space can become an issue by the time the third round rolls around. But we do view the first two rounds as roughly equivalent." – Bruce DelMonico, assistant dean and director of admissions at the Yale School of Management

"[We] get about a third of our applications in Round 1, about 55% in Round 2, and the remainder in Round 3…. We encourage people to submit their application when they feel that they offer their best possible applications…. So, if you can get everything lined up and completed and you feel really good about it…, then I would encourage you to apply in Round 1. But if it takes you a bit longer, and you want to take the time to look at your application again and maybe have somebody else look at it, then Round 2 is fine, too." – Soojin Kwon, director of admissions at the University of Michigan's Ross School of Business

"We look at statistics over the years—how many applications we got, how many we admitted and how many we yielded—and we try to even it out so we're not being too generous in one round at the expense of another round."
– Dawna Clarke, director of admissions at the Tuck School of Business at Dartmouth College

• •

Round 3

There is a misperception among candidates that being accepted to your target school is impossible if you apply in the third round. Although applying this late does make gaining acceptance quite challenging—schools have often filled 90%–95% of their classes by this time—logic would dictate that busy admissions officers have no reason to perpetrate a ruse on candidates by accepting hundreds of applications that they have no intention of reviewing. In short, the admissions offices accept Round 3 applications because they know excellent candidates are still out there and do not want to lose these individuals to other programs.

So, if you are a standout applicant, you can still succeed in Round 3 and can claim one of those few remaining places in the class for your own. Likewise, if you are a great applicant and represent a demographic that the school may be seeking, you also stand a chance of being accepted in Round 3. With respect to demographics, for most schools, Round 3 is a "shaping round," meaning that admissions officers are usually looking to balance the makeup of or identify "holes" in the class they are building and will pay special attention to those candidates who might help them achieve that balance or fill those holes: "Each year, we have five to ten candidates from Eastern Europe, and we only have two so far—let's keep our eyes open"; "Women usually make up 35% of our class, and we are at 30% now. Let's take a close look in this round"; "We don't have a teacher in the class yet!" Round 3 is not a good choice for the strategy consultant who has an average GPA and GMAT score and who just got too busy to apply earlier. This round is really only for you if you are an outstanding candidate overall or a strong applicant who offers some form of diversity.

• •

ADMISSIONS MYTHS DESTROYED: REAPPLICANTS SHOULD NOT REAPPLY

You applied to several MBA programs but were not accepted. The process took a lot of effort and caused a lot of heartache. Now what do you do? Applying to those schools again is not really an option, is it? They already rejected you once, so they will next time, right? WRONG.

MBA admissions committees are governed by self-interest. Simply put, the schools want the best candidates they can find. If you are among the best candidates, why would any admissions officer think, "Well, this is an outstanding candidate who can add something special to our school and has unique potential going forward, but he applied last year, so we'll just forget about him"? Indeed, the reapplication process is not a cruel practical joke on the part of the admissions committees or a disingenuous olive branch extended to those permanently on the outside. If business schools were not willing to accept any reapplicants, they would not invite applications from them and would certainly not waste time and resources reviewing those applications.

Although many candidates fret about being reapplicants, some admissions officers actually see the option of reapplying as a positive—as a new opportunity for both the applicant and the school. Soojin Kwon, director of admissions at the University of Michigan's Ross School of Business, told mbaMission, "They [reapplicants] are certainly not 'damaged goods.' We have had many successful reapplicants join our program after they've spent a year strengthening their candidacies."

And Bruce DelMonico, assistant dean and director of admissions at the Yale School of Management, echoed Kwon's sentiment, saying, "I can certainly bust that myth.... Our admit rate for reapplicants is actually the same as it is for first-time applicants. It's important, though, for reapplicants to explain to us how their candidacy has improved from the previous time they applied. Reapplicants need to make sure they enhance their application, rather than just resubmitting the same application."

Rod Garcia, senior director of admissions at the MIT Sloan School of Management, likewise feels that reapplicants are on equal footing with first-time candidates, asserting, "It is not a life sentence! Reapplicants do get in."

In short, then, if you are a reapplicant, you have no reason to believe that you have used and missed your one and only chance of attending your target business school. Like any competitive MBA applicant, continue to strive and achieve, and if things do not work out this time, there is always next time!

• •

Early Decision/Early Action

You may be wondering why we chose to address the early decision/early action application option at the *end* of this section, when clearly, the "early" nature of these rounds means that they precede even Round 1. The reason is that, at this point (the end of the 2012–2013 application season), few business schools have an application system that includes either one. Columbia Business School and Duke University's Fuqua School of Business are the only top MBA programs that offer special consideration of a candidate in exchange for that individual's binding commitment to attend their program, if accepted. Meanwhile, the Tuck School of Business at Dartmouth College offers an early application program in which accepted candidates from that round are required to pay a nonrefundable deposit within approximately one month of being admitted, but they are still able to apply to and consider other schools until that deposit is paid. So, if Columbia, Duke or Tuck is your first-choice school, we recommend that you consider applying early and getting that special consideration — but remember that this option comes with additional costs at Columbia and Duke.

YOUR MBA APPLICATION TIMELINE

PRE-STAGE

You should consider the time up until May of the year in which you plan to apply your pre-application period. Why? Because in May, the schools begin to release their all-important essay questions, and by mid-August, they have released the application forms (including résumé guidelines, recommendation requirements and more). By ensuring that you are well organized beforehand, you will be able to focus on your essays from your very first opportunity in May and then address your application more broadly from August until the end of Round 1 — as a result, you should be able to get all of your applications done by the first round deadline. So, what do you need to achieve during this pre-stage period?

Complete the GMAT

In an ideal world, you will have achieved your target (or optimal) GMAT score by May, so that you do not need to be working, studying for and taking the GMAT, writing essays, trying to maintain a social life and attending to any other responsibilities you may have all at once. Therefore, the *latest* date by which you should enroll in a GMAT course is December (of the year before the one in which you will apply). This will give you nine weeks to complete the course (through early February) and four weeks to study on your own (through early March) before taking the test the first time in early March and a second time in April. Following this schedule means you can take a weekend or two off after the second GMAT date and can start writing your essays in May!

Pursue Additional Coursework

If you plan to take additional courses to create an alternate transcript, as we discussed in Chapter 1, you should schedule your two classes so that they are complete by April or May—meaning that you need to be enrolled for a January term, at the latest. Your schedule will thereby be free starting in May. You may be thinking, "But you just suggested that I study for the GMAT during this time!" That is true, and this is precisely why we say that planning ahead is so important.

Ideally, you should not be working to build your alternate transcript while simultaneously studying for the GMAT, so that you can do your best on both tasks—earning those imperative As in your classes and achieving a high score on the GMAT. Focusing on one at a time will increase your chances for success. If you feel that you would benefit from taking additional classes first, you will need to head back to campus during the fall term, meaning in September of the year before the one in which you plan to apply. This will allow you to complete your course work by December, opening up your schedule so you can then leap into your GMAT study. If you plan to take the GMAT first, begin studying for the exam in September or earlier, so that you are done with the GMAT by December. Then you can enroll in January term classes and be done creating an alternate transcript by May. You can take these courses and the GMAT even earlier than these suggested dates, of course—we just recommend that you be done with both before May of your application year.

Contemplate School Choices and Visit Target Schools

With schools' essay questions coming out in May, most candidates do not realize that May is already too late to visit the full-time programs they are targeting. Because the academic year ends in May, schools' class visit programs wrap up by then—and do not start up again until late October. This means that applicants planning to apply in Round 1 will have to submit their applications before having the opportunity to sit in on a class at the school. Visiting your target programs and observing a class at each is valuable firsthand experience that will be crucial in establishing your "fit" with the school in your essays and interviews, so you must plan on accomplishing this well in advance of your application year. If at all possible, you should schedule a visit to your target schools between October and March.

At some schools, you will not earn any extra points for visiting. In particular, Harvard Business School and the University of Chicago Booth School of Business have been vocal on this point, stating that these visits are exclusively for the candidate's benefit. On the other hand, schools that are more off the beaten path, so to speak—such as Dartmouth Tuck in Hanover, New Hampshire, and Cornell's Samuel Curtis Johnson Graduate School of Management in Ithaca, New York—generally appreciate the effort applicants make in traveling to campus and so view such a visit quite favorably. At the same time, you can negatively identify yourself by *not* visiting a school if the trip involved is objectively not very taxing. For instance, if you live in New York City, you *must* visit New York University's Stern School of Business or Columbia Business School if you plan to apply; otherwise, you will give the impression that you are lazy or even uninterested.

Beyond ingratiating yourself to the admissions committee, though, visiting a school confers other direct benefits. Earning an MBA can be enormously expensive—from tuition to living costs to lost income and retirement savings, just to start—so you owe it to yourself to do your homework to ensure you are targeting schools that are best for you personally and for your career goals. With tuition for an MBA program costing as much as $58K per year for two years and living expenses being roughly $40K per year (lifestyle dependent), your business school experience could run as much as $200K when all is said and done, if not more—and we have not yet factored in two years of lost wages and retirement contributions. You likely would not spend tens of thousands of dollars on a new car without test driving it first, and business school should be no different. Would you not like to know what you are buying for hundreds of thousands of dollars before you commit to it?

Consider augmenting your process of discovery by meeting with your target school's alumni and students, so that you can gain a more in-depth understanding of these programs from the people who know it best. Most schools have ambassadorial programs through which you can connect with current students, and these students are typically aware of specific programs and classes that may not be prominently featured on a school's Web site or in its publications but that may appeal to you and even allow you to strengthen your case. To connect with alumni, you may have to employ your own network or otherwise do some investigating to find contacts, but the additional insight you will gain will be incredibly valuable. Although the alumni and student contacts you make will not be able to pull any strings to get you accepted, by communicating with them directly, you will collect a variety of useful data that you can then use to persuade the admissions committee that its school is ideally suited to you, in a way that few others will be able to do.

• •

ADMISSIONS MYTHS DESTROYED: ALUMNI GET YOU IN!

From time to time, we at mbaMission visit admissions officers at the top business schools, which gives us the opportunity to ask rather frank questions. On a visit to a top-five program, we pushed an admissions officer on the extent of alumni influence in the admissions process and ultimately received a surprising response: "We get ten letters each year from [a globally famous alumnus whose name mbaMission is withholding], telling us that this or that MBA candidate is the greatest thing since sliced bread. He gets upset when we don't admit 'his' applicants, but what makes him think that he deserves ten spots in our class?"

Many MBA applicants fret about their lack of alumni connection with their target schools, and the myth persists that admission to business school is about who you know, not who you are or what you can offer. Of course, these latter qualities are more important, and a standout applicant who knows no graduates at all from the school he or she is targeting is still a standout applicant and should get in—just as a weak applicant who knows a large number of alumni or a particularly well-known graduate is still a weak applicant and should not get in. Clearly, some extreme exceptions exist where influence can be exerted, but the "standard" applicant need not worry that every seat at the top MBA programs has already been claimed by someone with connections.

Remember, the admissions committees want to ensure that a diversity of ideas and experiences is represented in the classroom. Every top MBA class includes people from different socioeconomic backgrounds, nationalities, religions, professional backgrounds, ages, etc. Harvard has roughly 900 students in each incoming class, and the vast majority of these students do not personally know a CEO or the president of a country. And who knows? These days, such connections could even be a liability.

• •

Pursue Firm Sponsorship of Your MBA

If you plan to remain with (or return to) your current firm after you receive your MBA, you would be wise to do some research now on whether your firm will sponsor your degree. While the financial benefits of firm sponsorship are obvious, many prospective students do not realize that there is additional power inherent in being a firm-sponsored candidate. The admissions committees know that these applicants, with their firm's backing, will be employed upon graduation and that these individuals' post-MBA goals are thereby "guaranteed." Furthermore, the admissions committee will sleep better, knowing that when the school later reports its employment statistics to *Bloomberg Businessweek* as part of that publication's regular MBA ranking survey, the program will likely see a small benefit in the "percentage of candidates employed upon graduation" and possibly even "average starting salary" categories.

So, be sure to find out whether your firm has an MBA sponsorship program and if so, learn what is necessary to earn a firm scholarship. We have worked with clients who have needed to apply for such a scholarship within their company as early as a year and a half before their proposed MBA programs would begin; obviously, in such cases, you do not want to be broaching the subject at the last moment. Similarly, we have worked with clients whose firms did not originally have sponsorship programs but created them when our candidates brought forth the idea—a process that can involve months of bureaucratic haggling. This is therefore an option you should address as soon as possible.

Conduct Informational Interviews/Job Shadow

We always emphasize that candidates should strive to differentiate themselves from others via their experiences and the sincerity of their voice in their essays. With respect to sincerity, many candidates have trouble honestly articulating their post-MBA aspirations, and virtually every business school requires that candidates write an essay on short- and long-term career goals. If your plans involve entering a competitive field, such as banking or consulting, you should consider conducting informational interviews with someone in the industry or even job shadowing one or two for a day, if possible, so that you truly *know* what is involved in the role you claim to want after graduation. This kind of firsthand research absolutely must be done long before you write your goal statement and should *not* be left until you are ready to begin work on your essays. By taking this invaluable step early on, you can better avoid the networking and scheduling headaches that can arise and will be more prepared to focus on your application.

Identify Recommenders/Reconnect with Previous Supervisors

We find that one of the most frustrating parts of the application process for candidates is connecting with and motivating recommenders. Thus, you should take the time now—during the pre-stage phase—to identify your potential recommenders (even if you do not actually approach them for months) and gather some intelligence on each of them. Has your recommender written letters for anyone else? Is this person generous with his or her time with respect to employee feedback and review sessions? One of the best windows into your recommendation process will be the experiences of any colleagues for whom your target recommenders have already written such a letter; you may want to speak with these individuals to discover how your intended recommender managed their respective processes. By identifying recommenders who will be helpful and generous, you will potentially alleviate the stress of missed deadlines and unpredictable letters.

While you should spend time right now doing your homework on readily available recommenders, you should also take time to reconnect with previous supervisors who could also be strong recommenders, but with whom you have fallen out of touch. You do not want to find yourself in a position where you are calling a former supervisor for the first time in a year or more and asking him or her for a large chunk of time on a tight deadline. If you know you will need to call on a former supervisor, make contact with this individual now and keep the relationship warm for the next few months. You will be far better off when the letter-writing process begins.

Note: In most cases, MBA admissions committees have a bias toward current supervisors, but depending on the situation, past supervisors can be acceptable.

Prepare Your Résumé

Another simple step you can take now to help reduce competing interests later is preparing your résumé and then making small modifications and updates regarding your most recent position in October of your application year, during the latest stages of Round 1 and just before you officially submit your application. An added benefit is that you will start the process of reflecting on your accomplishments and thereby reawaken yourself to certain experiences. In many ways, preparing your résumé can act as a primer for your essay brainstorming process, which will be the foundation for your essays.

Advance Professional/Community/Personal Goals

Throughout the entire pre-stage portion of the application process, you should never stop striving toward your professional, community and personal goals. Your foot should remain squarely on the gas pedal with respect to these areas of your profile. By identifying opportunities to initiate, engage and lead in the months leading up to your application season, you will find that when you begin assembling your application and writing your essays, you will have a variety of dimensions you can showcase, a number of stories to draw from and a depth of experience that will appeal to admissions officers.

APPLICATION STAGE: MAY TO JANUARY

Brainstorm and Write Essays

By the time May rolls around, you should be ready to start actually applying, meaning you should have given a significant amount of thought to what you want to say as a candidate, and your knuckles should already be cracked so you can start typing as soon as your target schools release their essay questions.

You may be thinking, "Do I really need to start writing essays in May when they are not due until October?" In fact, yes, but this does not mean you must hammer away on your keyboard day after day until the deadline, yet crafting compelling essays takes time, patience and reflection. If you are like the average candidate and want to complete three to five applications, you may need to write five or six drafts of four to five essays per school, which means you could be writing up to 150 drafts of your essays within just a few short months. You should get the process started in May so that by June, you are in the thick of your essay writing, dedicating a few hours to it each workweek and significant time on weekends. You do not need to be a Pulitzer Prize–winning author to get into business school, but you do need to sincerely articulate your vision and reveal your unique potential through the stories you share. Accomplishing all this in just one marathon writing session is beyond challenging, if not outright impossible. Instead, take a slow-and-steady, more measured approach, and stick with it!

If you are like most applicants, you will likely aim to submit a few applications (perhaps three to four) in the first round and a few (perhaps one to two) in the second. In this case, your essay writing will stretch over several more months, starting in May and ending in January.

Note: We offer more than 50 free essay-writing tips on our blog: www.mbamission.com/blog.

Identify Your Target Schools

By the end of June, at the latest, most MBA programs will have released their essay questions for the coming year. So, by then, you should have started paring down your list of target schools and determined the ones to which you will apply in Round 1. Generally, we recommend that MBA aspirants who *must* start an MBA program the following year apply to five or six schools, targeting a mix of safe, competitive and reach programs. However, you should never sacrifice quality for quantity—apply only to the number of schools to which you can commit yourself entirely.

Meet with Your Recommenders

In some ways, you can never start too early meeting with your recommenders, discussing their important role in the application process and even reviewing your major accomplishments with them, so that these elements are fresh in their minds when they begin writing about you and your achievements.

To better understand why starting this portion of the application process sooner rather than later is so important, put yourself in the place of one of your potential recommenders. Imagine how you would feel if someone with whom you used to work suddenly called or emailed and said, "I need five detailed letters of recommendation done by next week, and each one is very different from the others. Can you write these for me?" Clearly, giving your recommenders some advance warning and plenty of time to complete their letters is very important. When the schools release their recommendation guidelines in August (or even earlier, in some cases), you should reach out to your recommenders—meeting with them in person, if possible—to ask them for their "blessing" and clearly explain the responsibilities of the task and the deadlines they need to meet.

Then you will need to follow up with them in September and early October (or as frequently as you feel is necessary) so that they do not miss Round 1 deadlines, and then in November and December if you are submitting applications in Round 2, so they do not miss those deadlines either. We have found that the best way to ensure that your recommenders complete their letters and forms on time is to present them with your own deadline, rather than the official one. For example, if the application to your target program is due on October 10, you could tell your recommenders that you must have the completed recommendation(s) by September 30. By setting this advanced deadline, you can put some mild pressure on any of your recommenders who fail to meet your accelerated deadline and have enough of a time cushion to avoid a major setback as a result (i.e., if this were to happen on the actual deadline day).

Complete the Short-Answer Sections

Many applicants will work painstakingly on their essays, prepare rigorously for their interviews and endlessly contemplate their choices of recommenders but leave completing the short-answer sections of their applications (the actual application forms) to the last moment—an approach we certainly do not recommend. Completing these sections can be very time-consuming, and they should be approached with the same seriousness and attention to detail that you give all the other parts of your application. You should therefore begin them early and strive to have them all done by mid-September. This will not only give you ample time to complete these sections properly, but also free up your time and focus closer to the submission deadline(s) so you can address any other aspects of your application that are more painstaking—usually the essays.

Complete and Submit First-Round Applications

As you approach the first-round application deadlines, you should, of course, do whatever you can to submit your best work. Once you have submitted your application, though, you should mentally let the process go. If you later realize that some part of your application included a typo, this is unfortunate, but it is not a reason to panic. Admissions committees are not looking for reasons to reject you; they are seeking to get to know you through your files. So, press submit, and start looking ahead rather than backward. If you plan to submit more applications in Round 2, consider first giving yourself a short break of approximately one week to clear your head and recharge before tackling that second round. The application process can be exhausting, and you will need to be at your best to compete.

Plan First-Round Interviews

In some cases, you will be able to schedule your own interview with your target school. In other cases, the admissions committee will read your application and invite you to interview. (We discuss the different types of interviews in depth in Chapter 9.) Either way, the bottom line is that you should have your first-round interviews completed by November or early December. Then, all you can do is wait for your school to let you know its decision.

Receive First-Round Decisions

Schools will start announcing first-round decisions in December and will continue to do so into January. Some will release decisions all at once online, whereas others will slowly release them via phone calls or online over a period of a few weeks. If your friend hears from a school before you, do not panic. The timing of the school's response indicates nothing about your chances for acceptance. Definitely avoid the temptation to call the admissions office and ask whether a decision has been made about your candidacy. Admissions personnel are easily frustrated by such calls and will not give you the answers you seek. Sit back, try to be patient and the school will contact you in due time.

In most cases, you will get a notification of either "admit" or the less welcome "reject" (though the schools will not be this blunt). Another possibility is that you will receive a notification of "indecision," meaning that you have been placed on the school's waitlist—quite a frustrating turn of events, but no cause for pessimism. Being waitlisted is actually a positive sign, indicating that your target school does not want to miss out on the option of admitting you, though it is not yet ready to do so. When you are placed on the waitlist, your target school's admissions director will likely send you a letter about the waitlist process. You must read this letter very carefully and follow the school's instructions precisely. In some cases, you will need to indicate whether you want to remain on the waitlist or withdraw yourself from consideration, and sometimes the school will invite you to submit additional information—or specifically note that no supplemental information should be provided. If you find yourself on a school's waitlist, the game is hardly over, and in some cases, the indecision may linger until the week before the MBA program is scheduled to begin. Some schools continue to admit students until the very last moment, so be prepared to work on your patience. (If you find yourself on a school's waitlist, be sure to consult Appendix C, "The Waitlist," for guidance on managing this phase of the application process.)

Submit Second-Round Applications

If you plan to submit applications in the second round, these will be due in most cases by mid-January. As we noted earlier, you should strive to make Round 2 your final application round. Although the admissions "party" is not over for everyone at the end of the second round, hopefully it is for you. Your applications should all be done, and perhaps you have even been notified of an acceptance or two from your first-round applications, so you can start getting back to normal. Like many candidates, you may feel that the application process has ruled your life for the previous few months and now you suddenly find yourself with a ton of free time. Take a moment to breathe and enjoy it until second-round interviews roll around.

Receive Second-Round Interview Invitations and Decisions

Second-round interview invitations should begin trickling out by the end of January, followed by a wave of invitations in February and a few more in March. Usually by March, schools will start announcing second-round decisions and will continue into April. Ideally, you have been diligent with your applications and balanced ambition and optimism with realistic expectations. We hope that at this point, you will be popping the champagne and getting ready to begin earning your MBA at a top business school of your choice.

Submit Third-Round Applications and Interview

Clearly, we recommend applying to your target school(s) in the first or second round to increase your chances for admission, but if you *must* apply to a top school in the third round, then certainly do so. However, if you started your MBA application process with a robust "pre-stage," by now you may feel like you have given your entire life over to this endeavor. Stay focused, and by March or April, your applications will all be submitted, and your interviews will be scheduled in April or May. Hopefully, you will be the standout applicant who is successful in this late round!

POST-APPLICATION

Attend Admitted Students Weekend

Many schools schedule a single weekend wherein all admitted students are invited to campus to meet their potential classmates, socialize with one another and with enrolled students and faculty and get to know the school even better. These weekend events often take place in February or April, prior to deposit deadlines (discussed in the following section). We strongly encourage you to attend your target school's admitted student weekend if you are invited to do so and if at all possible, because it will help inform your final decision. Admissions officers know that many admitted applicants use the weekend to delve more deeply into the MBA experience at the school and wait till after to decide which program to attend. Understandably, the schools put on their best faces during these events in hopes that you bond with your prospective classmates and form a stronger identification with the school. Suddenly, the tables have turned, and *you* are evaluating *them*!

Submit Your Deposit

A few weeks or months after you have been accepted to a program, you will need to pay a deposit to secure your place in the class. Deposit dates vary from school to school, but most first-round deposit deadlines are in late February or early March, and second-round deposit deadlines in late April or early May. If you submitted applications in both Round 1 and Round 2, you may be required to submit a deposit for a program that accepted you in the first round to hold your spot, or to diplomatically request an extension so you have time to find out how you did in Round 2 before committing to a school. Deposits are frequently a few thousand dollars, and although no one likes to risk that kind of money, if you are uncertain which program to choose once your options are clear, paying a school's deposit can buy you a little extra time to make this important life decision.

Apply for Scholarships/Student Loans

Most schools award scholarships at the same time they admit a candidate, and some give you the chance to write yet another (!) essay—or two—to apply for these awards. Despite your likely fatigue at this point in the process, you should muster the energy to write these scholarship essays. Business schools can be quite generous with financial aid, and applying for scholarships and student loans is pretty straightforward. Your letter of acceptance will usually include information on whom to contact in the school's financial aid office, and someone should shepherd you through the process.

Start the Visa Process

If you are not a U.S. citizen, you will need to apply for a student visa, and processing it can take time. Fortunately, your chosen school will assist you with the process, which tends to be more bureaucratic than difficult. As long as you submit your application early, you should have your visa in hand long before your first day at the school.

Quit Your Job

Once admitted, most applicants have a rare opportunity to take a riskless and extended vacation. If you find yourself in this position, you should definitely take time off before business school. Once things start rolling in late July or early August (with moving, orientation, etc.), your life will become quite busy and intense as you juggle classes, club activities and responsibilities, the demands of recruiting, socializing and so on. Perhaps we should end this chapter right here before we extend this timeline too far…

CHAPTER 3

BRAINSTORMING

Brainstorming

The goal of brainstorming before beginning to write your MBA application essays is to identify not just the experiences, but more importantly, the stories that make you distinct from other business school applicants. Conveying your past responsibilities and the nature of your work, volunteer efforts and personal accomplishments to the admissions committee is essential, and the most effective way of doing this is by telling stories about them—each with a beginning, middle and end. To help you as you begin to contemplate your stories and uncover them one at a time, we have created a questionnaire, provided later in this chapter, that will serve as a guide.

Professional Experiences

Admissions committees judge your professional experiences not on the basis of the dollars involved, but on your actions. Whether you are describing how you helped merge two multibillion-dollar firms or how you started a local bicycle shop, the admissions committee is more concerned with the intensity of your spirit than with a monetary value. Factual aspects of the experiences you describe provide context, but the emotional aspects are what give your stories power. No matter how "small" an experience might seem, if you brought the entirety of your passion and creativity to it, the admissions committee should find it compelling.

Although professional stories typically involve traditional business accomplishments (e.g., closing a deal, finding a new market niche), your "soft" achievements in the workplace can also be worthy fodder for compelling essays. By "soft," we mean the more human, perhaps less quantifiable aspects of your professional experiences, such as developing and implementing a mentorship program for interns, founding a workplace improvement committee or helping a struggling colleague. These stories can sometimes be extremely powerful and set you apart from the crowd.

Community/Volunteer Stories

Likewise, give sincere consideration to any "hard" accomplishments you achieved as part of your community activities. These can just as effectively prove your competencies and, more importantly, diversify your application and highlight your personal values. For example, you could tell the story of how you managed a successful fundraiser for a local charity, coached a children's soccer team or helped an elderly neighbor with her taxes and financial planning. Although the scale of the accomplishment(s) may or may not be in proportion to your work achievements, scale is not what is relevant. The admissions committee is more concerned with your spirit, actions and decision-making ability.

Personal Stories

Many MBA applicants will overlook their personal accomplishments entirely, mistakenly determining that business schools only want to learn about their core business skills and talents. However, personal stories have the potential to powerfully differentiate you from other candidates. You alone can claim your personal accomplishments—no one else can or will tell the same stories. For example, one candidate with whom we worked learned Spanish just to be able to read a book his great-grandfather wrote in his native tongue, while another helped house and educate a dislocated refugee—both applicants have distinct and fascinating stories to tell that lie outside the realm of traditional professional and community accomplishments. These might be unique examples, but most likely, at some point, you have gone above and beyond to help another person or to push yourself. These kinds of stories are remarkably valuable and should definitely not be ignored.

Admissions Myths Destroyed: I Am a Simple Product!

Many candidates worry that they cannot express their stories in a single sentence or that their personal branding is too muddled. Some feel that they must have a single narrative and continuously speak to it to make a point with the admissions committees. But you are not a simple product with just one or two worthwhile attributes—a Budweiser beer, for example, which can be fully represented with just the straightforward slogan "The Great American Lager." MBA candidates are far more complex than consumer products, of course. So, presenting yourself as one-dimensional ("I am an entrepreneur in everything I do," "I am a finance guy") is indeed a mistake—and one that prevents you from revealing your depth of character and experience.

Let us consider a basic example: Jon built a lawn care business and grew it from a single-truck enterprise into a ten-truck business, and he also coached Little League baseball, becoming a de facto "big brother" to one of the kids on the team. Why should Jon show the admissions committee only his entrepreneurial side and ignore his empathetic and altruistic treatment of the young baseball player? Why would Jon not reveal his depth and versatility instead, telling both stories and revealing distinct but complementary strengths?

At mbaMission, we encourage candidates to brainstorm thoroughly and consider each of their stories from as many different angles as possible. There is no simple formula for presenting yourself to the admissions committee. In fact, showing that you are a multitalented and sophisticated person is quite important.

After all, admissions committees are on the hunt for the next great business leaders, and a truly dynamic candidate—like you!—cannot be described in just a few words.

• •

THE BRAINSTORMING PROCESS

When you are brainstorming, "more is more" is definitely the rule. A compelling story is obviously the foundation of a profound essay, so the more exploration you do and the more stories you uncover—and can thus consider for inclusion in your essays—the more likely you are to pinpoint the most effective options. We do not advise choosing a weak story and trying to make it compelling through the shrewd use of language. And do not confuse "weak story" with "unsuccessful result"—some candidates' most powerful essays are about times when they actually did *not* reach their goals or struggled significantly with something. Be exhaustive. Spend many hours brainstorming, and consider all the facets of your life. This up-front investment will pay dividends throughout your application process.

Also, as you brainstorm, try to consider each of your experiences from multiple angles. For example, the brand manager who brought a new product to market may think of this accomplishment as an example of leadership only, but the story can actually be used to illustrate several other aspects of the candidate's experiences. The brand manager may have conceived the idea (creativity) and pushed his or her firm to implement it (entrepreneurship), managed a staff and navigated internal conflicts (teamwork skills), dealt with sourcing issues or product attributes (ethics), struggled along the path to success (failure/setbacks), etc. Do not accept your stories merely at face value, but take time to explore what they might represent in broader terms. (For more guidance, see the "Viewing a Story from Different Angles" section of Chapter 9.)

Your brainstorming process is not necessarily exclusive to your own memory. Consider discussing your experiences with parents, supervisors, colleagues, friends and other appropriate individuals to generate additional stories and even discover how others view(ed) you and your accomplishments. Simply put, sometimes you may be unaware of instances in which you have shone, and other people may see a quality or skill in you that you did not realize you possessed. These added perspectives can help create a fuller, richer picture for you to work with going forward.

Using the questionnaire that follows as a guide, write down everything that comes to mind in response to the various prompts. Although there is no "right" page length for your brainstorming document, most candidates tend to exhaust themselves somewhere between 10 and 15 pages.

Brainstorming Questionnaire

1. List your major accomplishments/achievements (not responsibilities!) in each of your professional positions (see the example that follows). To the best of your ability, briefly describe the beginning, middle and end of what would constitute a story about these accomplishments.

<u>Example</u>

Company/Dates of Employment: *Foremost Recruiting Associates Inc.; Sept. 2009–Present*

Company Description (if company is not well known, be brief!): *Foremost is a 300-person human resources consulting firm, operating out of Kansas City, Kansas.*

Department: *Corporate Recruiting*

Job Title: *Senior Consultant*

Accomplishment 1: *Established new accounting recruitment department*

- Beginning: *Approached management with idea to enter accounting recruitment market; persuaded management to dedicate human resources and $120K budget*

- Middle: *Managed staff of three; identified 80 credible candidates; held unique marketing events/career fairs to showcase candidates; aggressively built relationships with 60 manufacturers in tristate area*

- End: *Placed 37 candidates in first year; revenue of $420K; promoted; budget increased and additional human resources allocated*

Accomplishment 2: …

- Beginning: …

- Middle: …

- End: …

2. List your major accomplishments in each of your community activities, following a similar format (template below).

Example

Organization/Dates of Involvement: *Urban Kitchen; July 2010–Present*

Description of Organization: *Urban Kitchen aggregates unserved restaurant meals and provides this food to the less fortunate*

Role: *Shift Coordinator*

Hours Per Month: *16*

Accomplishment 1: *Raised funds for full-time general manager*

- Beginning: *Saw organization being stretched; identified need for general manager to recruit volunteers and oversee distribution*

- Middle: *Networked with existing corporate sponsors; identified available government grants; applied for grants from charitable foundations*

- End: *Received $55K in funding; full-time manager in place; 12 new volunteers are serving 15% more meals per week*

3. List your major accomplishments in each of your collegiate extracurricular activities, following the format shown in the examples for Questions 1 and 2.

4. List any instances in which you have made a significant difference in another human being's life (e.g., helping solve a family problem, teaching a child to read, mentoring a coworker who is having trouble, etc.).

5. List the five personal accomplishments of which you are most proud (as they relate to yourself, not others—e.g., completed a marathon, published a poem in literary journal, overcame a fear of heights, traveled to 17 different countries, etc.).

6. List your academic accomplishments: awards, honors, distinctions, publications, etc. Briefly explain the nature of and selection criteria for each.

7. List any professional/community recognition that has been bestowed upon you.

8. a) Describe any particularly rewarding relationships that you have had or b) any conflicts you have dealt with in professional or organizational settings and how you handled them.

9. Discuss any professional or personal setbacks or failures that you have experienced (not addressed in Question 8). Have you ever missed any opportunities, not achieved a goal or disappointed another person?

10. List your primary hobbies and interests, past and present.

11. List five words or phrases your friends/family would use to describe you. List five words or phrases you would use to describe yourself.

12. List all the countries to which you have traveled and your reason for doing so (i.e., business or pleasure).

13. List any language(s) you speak aside from your native tongue and your level of fluency in each.

14. Briefly, what are your short-term and long-term goals after business school?

15. List the reasons you feel you want/need to get an MBA. How do you believe an MBA program will prepare you to reach your goals, and why do you believe now is the best time to get this degree?

16. What do you want to learn in an MBA program? What will be your area of focus?

17. Is there *anything* else you feel you should share?

CHAPTER 4

ESSAY WRITING

Essay Writing

Part I: Preparing Outlines for Your Essays

Years of experience have proven to us that virtually every candidate is better off creating outlines for his or her essays before writing the first full drafts. You are a busy person—you are balancing work, studying for and taking the GMAT, engaging in community activities, trying to maintain a personal life and more. Why not bring some efficiency and organization to the essay writing process?

Truth be told, some applicants' first reaction to the concept of creating an outline rather than simply diving into writing a first draft is not a positive one. They imagine that this "extra" step will add time and complicate their application process when in fact, creating an outline can not only help streamline one's essay writing but can also go a long way in boosting the resulting essays' effectiveness. By taking the time to first organize your thoughts in the form of short phrases and key terms, you will see that your story unfolds more easily and will be able to ensure that no gaps occur in the information you are trying to convey. This means a stronger, more persuasive final essay and, in most cases, fewer rounds of editing and revision.

The Outline as Roadmap

Think of your outline as a kind of roadmap, one that guides you smoothly from the beginning of your story to the end, noting each important milestone along the way. Each major heading—or, if you prefer, each bullet point—should therefore consist of a very brief summary of a bigger idea. In other words, it should capture your key point but not include the background, explanation or descriptive details, leaving those for the first draft of the essay. Your outline should simply provide a concise overview of what you intend to write in your essay.

When constructing your outline, you can use very informal language, and you do not need to worry about using full sentences or proper grammar. After all, you are not submitting your outline to anyone—it is for "internal use only," so to speak. In general, we recommend that your outline be no longer than approximately 50% of the total word count allowed for the essay. Outlining a 500-word essay with eight bullet points of 100 words each is pointless—your outline would be longer than your final essay, and this would not facilitate a more organized, efficient or enjoyable writing experience.

THE SUPER SUMMARY

Your first step in outlining any essay is to compose one very clear sentence that captures the key idea that ties your entire essay together. This "super summary" of your essay will allow you to focus your thoughts and structure your work, much like a thesis sentence would for a more scientific or theoretical text. This is a nuanced but important point: for your business school application essays, you are not attempting to use a thesis to "prove" a point factually but are trying to construct a narrative that illustrates a central idea or experience from your life. So, before you begin writing, you may prepare a rigidly structured outline and a straightforward statement of your central point, but when you present these elements in essay form, you will need to make them softer and less explicit.

In Sample Essay A, which appears in full later in this section, the candidate is answering the question "Describe an impact you have had on an individual, group or organization. How has this experience been valuable to you or others? (500 words)." As you will see, the applicant has chosen to write about his experience as a volunteer children's soccer coach. A good super summary for this essay might then be: "Through creative motivational techniques and enthusiastic leadership, I helped maintain the spirits of a group of 12-year-old boys during a soccer season in which they lost almost all their games."

This super summary works well because it presents the structure of the entire essay in one concise sentence. You now know exactly what the essay is going to discuss (the writer's challenging experience as a children's soccer coach one season) and how the essay will be focused.

BREAKING IT DOWN

Building on the super summary, the candidate could then generate a structure for the essay by identifying the content to be presented in each of its key paragraphs, as follows:

Super Summary: "Through creative motivational techniques and enthusiastic leadership, I helped maintain the spirits of a group of 12-year-old boys during a soccer season in which they lost almost all their games."

- *Paragraph 1*: Introduction to the challenges encountered with the team

- *Paragraph 2*: Preventative actions taken to resolve these challenges

- *Paragraph 3*: Motivational actions taken to resolve these challenges

- *Paragraph 4*: Results of the actions taken

- *Paragraph 5*: Lessons learned ("Takeaways")

Next, to create a logical and defined structure for these paragraphs, the candidate can add some short bullet points to the base outline to support the central idea within each one, as shown:

Paragraph 1: Introduction to the challenges encountered with the team

- I inherited a kids' soccer team that had lost all its games in the previous season; knew I was facing an uphill battle

- Noticed low morale immediately; after we lost the first five games of the season, things got worse

- Saw parents yelling at each other and at referees

- Recognized that situation needed to change

Paragraph 2: Preventative actions taken to resolve these challenges

- Held parent meeting to propose positive attitudes

- Took difficult step and asked one abusive parent to leave the next game

Paragraph 3: Motivational actions taken to resolve these challenges

- No team wins, so I rewarded small victories on team

- Gave each player a nickname so that soccer was a special activity for them

- Gave post-game and post-practice award to "hardest working player"

Paragraph 4: Results of the actions taken

- Negative parents stayed away; kids felt less pressure

- Players started showing up for practice on time, listened more, more energetic on and off the field, began to have real fun and learn

- Won four of our six final games that season

- Was asked to coach the following year

Paragraph 5: Lessons learned ("Takeaways")

- Usually very goal oriented, I became entirely process oriented; found rewards in my players' small victories

- Learned lessons in consistency and integrity

Once this has been done, writing the corresponding essay becomes much less difficult. Here we present the final essay, with comments that illustrate how it follows the candidate's outline.

Sample Essay A

"Describe an impact you've had on an individual, group or organization. How has this experience been valuable to you or others?" (500 words)

When Dr. Gibson, the parent of a child on the soccer team I had agreed to coach, handed me his whistle and said, "Good luck with the kids, but more so with the parents," I finally understood the true challenge before me.[1] A new season was starting, but my team of 12-year-olds would have difficulty forgetting the last, in which they lost 26 of 28 games. Even worse, we lost our first five games, so players started showing up late, parents began criticizing one another's kids and one parent stormed the field to confront a referee. Stunned, I knew I needed to take decisive action to reign in the chaos and salvage the season.[2]

First, I held a parents' meeting during which I outlined a zero-tolerance policy: "Only encouragement from the sidelines" and "Each player will arrive 15 minutes before game time to prepare or will not play." Admittedly, as a 24-year-old, I was uncomfortable enforcing rules with adults double my age,

---

1 While the writer is following the structure of the outline, he is also clearly adding color to it from the very first word. Thus, the outline serves its purpose as a structural foundation and not a mini essay.

2 The narrative structure of this essay belies the need for a definitive and "scientific" thesis statement. At the end of the broader introduction, the reader clearly understands the direction that the essay will take, but some mystery remains as to how the story will unfold.

but I knew I had to remain firm. At our next game, I demanded that a referee remove an abusive fan—one of my players' parents! I also refused to let a player who had arrived 20 minutes late play. After enforcing these rules, I did not have another such problem again.[3]

With the parents "tamed," I began working on the players. I had to find new ways to make soccer fun. I started giving my players nicknames. Soon, our team consisted of "Sparky," "Lefty," "Red" and others—names that brought smiles to the kids' faces, even when we were losing. Then, I decided that after each practice and game, I would announce a "hardest working player" award. As expected, players competed aggressively for the title, as each was motivated to earn the recognition. Throughout the next few games, I ensured that different players got the award, which created a sense of pride and positive spirit.[4]

With this new attitude and dedication, and negativity a thing of the past, I managed to run more drills and plan strategies in practice—which now began on time. Soon, my team was passing the ball more, and players were staying in their positions. Suddenly, we won a game; everyone celebrated as though we had won the World Cup! Then, we won a few more—four of our final six! At the season's end, the parents asked that I coach the team again the next season. Of course, I accepted.[5]

From elementary school through college, I had always played soccer with true competitors and focused on winning. I was surprised I could take pride in watching two 12-year-olds pass the ball well, even if they ultimately lost it to a player on the other team. I felt a strong sense of ownership over those passes. No matter what I have experienced in my professional career, my greatest test

---

3 Following the outline, the writer uses the ideas that he has already developed and now brings in the details to create the essay's personality.

4 Again, the writer incorporates into this paragraph the points specified in the outline, but he adds significant detail to flesh out these actions and truly paint a picture for the reader.

5 In this paragraph, we see a slight but reasonable deviation from the outline. That the negative parents stayed away is not *explicitly* stated here, but this change is implied in the writer's statement that negativity was "a thing of the past" at this point.

has been remaining stern with my team's parents—I learned lessons in consistency and integrity that will remain with me throughout my life.[6]

An outline should serve as a simple guide for writing a narrative, not dictate the essay's definitive and inalterable structure. If, while composing Sample Essay A, the writer had thought of a new takeaway or felt that the essay was taking shape in a slightly different way, that would be fine—the writer would simply need to revise the outline accordingly, ensuring that the revised outline still worked as a roadmap, effectively guiding the reader from the beginning of the story to the end, and that all the key milestones along the way made sense within context. The overarching idea here is to use the outline to get organized and to start in the right direction with a clear foundation.

UNCONVENTIONAL ESSAYS

In recent years, admissions officers have been begun incorporating a variety of what we call unconventional essays into their applications. The somewhat unusual formats and angles of these unorthodox essays serve two purposes: to elicit a better sense of candidates' true personalities and to reduce the likelihood that candidates will submit an essay they wrote for another school rather than investing the necessary time and effort into writing one specifically for the program in question. We use the term "essays" in reference to these application components, but in fact, these submissions can sometimes be PowerPoint presentations, audio files, video files or some other medium. Here are a few examples of unusual essay prompts:

- **New York University's Stern School of Business, 2012:** Please describe yourself to your MBA classmates. You may use almost

---

6 A philosophical conclusion can be challenging to outline, but the basic bullet points in our writer's outline are included here and simply expanded upon a bit. Obviously, the outline served well as a foundation for the essay.

any method to convey your message (e.g., words, illustrations). Feel free to be creative. If you submit a non-written piece for Essay 3 (i.e., artwork or multimedia) or if you submit Essay 3 via mail, please upload a brief description of your submission with your online application.

- **The University of Chicago's Booth School of Business, 2012:** The Chicago experience will take you deeper into issues, force you to challenge assumptions, and broaden your perspective. In a four-slide presentation or an essay of no more than 600 words, broaden our perspective about who you are. Understanding what we currently know about you from the application, what else would you like us to know?

- **The University of Michigan's Ross School of Business, 2012:** Introduce yourself to your future Ross classmates in 100 words or less.

- **Northwestern University's Kellogg School of Management, 2012:** What one interesting or fun fact would you want your future Kellogg classmates to know about you? (25 words or less)

- **The Johnson Graduate School of Management at Cornell University, 2012:** You are the author for the book of Your Life Story. Please write the Table of Contents for the book. (400 words)

Creating outlines for unconventional essays is just as important as it is for traditional essays—if not more so—and this step should not be skipped just because what you will be writing may be shorter than a regular essay or will not actually be written at all. No matter what medium you expect to use, you should thoroughly consider the content you want to convey before devising how you wish to present it.

One distinctive thing about many of the unconventional questions is that they are far more open-ended than typical essay prompts. A traditional essay question might be something like "What do you consider your most important leadership experience and what did you learn from it?" Clearly, such a question allows you to discuss only one anecdote selected from a rather narrow subject area. In contrast, the Chicago Booth prompt we presented earlier in this section ends by asking, "What else would you like us to know?" This much broader query allows you to consider endless possibilities and choose whatever you feel will help you truly stand out.

When preparing your response to an unconventional prompt, first think about what you have already shared with the admissions committee in the other parts of your application. Then, go through your brainstorming document and make note of *everything* you have not yet been able to include. You will not ultimately be able to cover *all* of this material in your unconventional essay (so please do not try!), but you will likely realize that you have a lot more material to work with than you originally thought. The following is a brainstorming list created by a candidate seeking to respond to New York University's (NYU's) Stern School of Business's Essay 3 prompt ("Please describe yourself to your MBA classmates.")—a list that ultimately served as his outline:

- Passion for lacrosse—coaching and playing

- Volunteer activities with New York Cares—serving at soup kitchen each weekend

- Love of *Star Wars* films and all films, for that matter

- Student government leadership at Duke

- Managing literature conference at Duke

- Love of biking—biking to work and Sunday bike rides with "team"

- Junior year abroad in France—continued dedication to French language study over the past two years and immersion week

- Mentorship of twin brothers

- Travel to 21 countries—Iceland, Russia and Peru highlights

- Close relationship with grandma

- Budding love of cooking

- Love of New York and my neighborhood in particular

NYU Stern Essay 3. Personal Expression

Please describe yourself to your MBA classmates. You may use almost any method to convey your message (e.g., words, illustrations). Feel free to be creative. If you submit a written essay, it should be 500 words maximum, double-spaced, 12-point font.

Recently, my college-aged twin brothers stayed in my New York apartment while I was away. I left them this note:

"Guys—*Mi casa es su casa*, but make sure *su casa* still looks like *mi casa* when I get back Saturday. And do not ride my bike! There's pizza in the fridge, or you can grab a bite around the corner. Call my cell if you need anything. Don't forget—you're coming with me Sunday! –Jonah"

The note I really wanted to leave, though, would have looked more like this:

"Guys—*Mi casa es su casa*, but make sure *su casa* still looks like *mi casa* when I get back. I know you'll probably defame my Blue Devils poster, but I'll just get a new one as soon as I get back. Remember, I'll be visiting you at UNC next month and will have the last laugh—your beloved Tar Heels aren't even ranked these days!

Please do not ride my bike. As you know, I bike to work each day and 60 miles through Palisades Park each weekend. As you may *not* know, it took me two years to save for that bike, and my neighbor's was just stolen. I don't let it out of my sight (but I know you will!). You can use my lacrosse gear, but don't toss the ball around inside. I shoved it all in the hall closet after Friday's practice. (My 12-year-olds are getting better every game—thanks for asking!) My helmet is almost as old as you and smells like it, too, so open the closet at your own risk.

I made pizza in my cooking class two nights ago—it's in the fridge. I know you typically prefer pepperoni to artichokes and sundried tomato, but I'm pretty sure you'll like it, so dig in.

I know you rarely take my recommendations, but if you'd rather go out, my favorite New York slice (after trying 30 spots!) is John's on Bleecker. For coffee, I go around the corner to Brew each morning. The staff is surly, but the coffee is second to none. For a cheap, spicy dinner, try Pho-Yeah! It's by the theater, which is showing some great documentaries and classics this week—check it out. (Use my loyalty card to get the frequent viewer discount.) If you go to the *Star Wars* screening, expect to see Chewbacca and Darth Vader in line for tickets. Sorry I don't have a Luke costume to lend you, despite my love for the trilogy.

My cell phone works in Morocco, so call if you need anything. I'll be in an immersion week in Fes. Mock me if you want, but I'll respond *en Français*. I get home Saturday and will head to the soup kitchen at the usual time on Sunday. Don't forget—I signed you guys up to work the shift with me. I will deflate your air mattresses if I have to. They are counting on you, and so am I. –Jonah."

PART II: WRITING EFFECTIVE ESSAYS

Even for the most practiced of writers, crafting a successful application essay can be challenging. Brainstorming and then organizing your thoughts into outlines for your essays will facilitate this process, as we illustrated in Part 1 of this chapter, and now we will offer a few basic rules that will help you create and refine your drafts. At the end of this chapter, we present a number of sample essays that illustrate these rules—but resist the urge to skip forward to them just yet!

Rule 1: Do Not Just Write an Essay—Write a Narrative

As we mentioned earlier in this chapter, you are not trying to "prove" a theory in your application essays (as you might have done in high school or college) but are instead trying to present a story that shows who you are and what you have experienced. You should therefore focus on narrative writing (which primarily describes) rather than expository writing (which primarily explains). In a narrative, the central facts about a situation are not just bluntly introduced, but are presented in a way that lets them speak for themselves and paint a rounded picture of an experience.

Consider the following examples:

Example 1

A: *"Ice hockey is a national passion and way of life in Canada. As a Canadian, I have been playing hockey constantly since I was three years old, when I laced up my skates for the first time. Each year throughout my youth, my father would build an ice rink in our back yard, where I would spend countless hours playing and practicing hockey."*

B: *"When I turned three, my grandmother bought me my first pair of ice skates, which I refused to take off—even when I went to bed at night—for the next full week. After two years of what my father now refers to as 'constant begging,' I managed to convince him to build a full-size ice rink in our back yard."*

Example 2

A: *"I love to travel and have visited more than 20 countries on four continents, primarily in Latin America, where I became fluent in Spanish and Portuguese."*

B: *"Peru, Ecuador, Columbia, Brazil and Argentina—after six months in these countries, I found myself joking good-naturedly and exchanging travel stories with the locals in colloquial Spanish and Portuguese."*

Within these two example sets, which statements create a more compelling image of the person you are reading about? Which ones paint a picture that you can visualize? We expect that for both examples, you selected the latter! When you take a narrative approach in your essays rather than simply presenting information outright, your writing evokes imagery for your reader, which is more compelling and gives him or her a stronger sense of who you are and what you have done.

Rule 2: Use the First Person

In your business school "essays" (errrr... narratives!), you should be writing from *your* perspective—meaning, writing in "first person." Returning to Example 1 in the previous section, consider the sentence "Ice hockey is a national passion and a way of life in Canada." This is a statement of fact that focuses on things other than the writer, in this case, ice hockey. Because you are talking about yourself and your experiences in your narratives, you should virtually always be using the pronouns "I," "me" and "my," rather than "one," "he" and "his," like we see in the second sentence in Example B: "When I turned three, my grandmother bought me my first pair of ice skates, which I refused to take off—even when I went to bed at night—for the next full week."

This first-person perspective imbues this sentence with a sense of owner-ship, which is absent in the first. "Ice hockey is a national passion and a way of life in Canada" is not a statement that applies exclusively to the writer or presents things from his point of view. In fact, this objec-tive statement could be made by just about anyone who knows anything about hockey or Canada, even if the writer has no personal connection whatsoever to either one. In contrast, that many people would share the exact same experience of having had their grandmother buy them skates when they were three and then wearing them nonstop for an entire week is very improbable—which means the chances of two people both writing the sentence "When I turned three, my grandmother bought me my first pair of ice skates, which I refused to take off—even when I went to bed at night—for the next full week" are almost nil. By creating truly personal sentences based on your particular experience and presenting them in the first person, you alone *own* the story, and this can help set you apart from the competition when you are applying to business school.

Rule 3: Keep Things Simple

If you have any concerns at this point that a narrative approach might be difficult to execute, let us reassure you that it is actually quite easy, because it allows you to simply consider and convey actual events and ex-periences as they occurred. As long as you have a strong story in mind, all you need to do is describe and reveal the sequence of events involved. To do this, you can continuously ask yourself, "And then what happened?" and generally, you should be able to keep reporting the action as it hap-pened.

Writing a narrative does not require using long, complex sentences or complicated or obscure vocabulary. In fact, the more straightforward your language, the easier telling your story will be. Consider the follow-ing sample sentences:

A: *When Dr. Gibson, the parent of a child on the soccer team I had agreed to coach, handed me his whistle and said, "Good luck with the kids, but more so with the parents," I finally understood the true challenge before me.*

B: *Dr. Gibson, bewildered and frantic, reluctantly turned over his whistle to me. Tears glimmering in his mournful eyes, he tremulously and resignedly uttered, "Good luck with the kids, but more so with the parents." Never before had I faced a challenge so daunting and unforgiving, yet seductive.*

Both lines are certainly very descriptive and evoke an image, but the first is straightforward and clear, whereas the second is so overloaded and complicated as to be ridiculous!

Rule 4: Connect the Dots

In an effective narrative essay, each sentence serves as a crucial link in the story. Removing a line would therefore leave the reader confused, because important information would be missing. To illustrate, we have eliminated a sentence from the following excerpt (from sample essay 2, which appears in full at the end of this chapter):

I joined the board of the BlackJack Theatre Company three weeks after a failed audit and the executive director's (ED's) surprise resignation. I was stunned to learn that only 12 chose not to do so and that 30 actually donated to the "save the theatre" campaign I had initiated.

Because we removed what was previously the second sentence, the paragraph is now confusing and the story difficult to follow. Any reader would suddenly wonder, "Twelve who? And chose not to do what?" Clearly, the information conveyed in the sentence that was removed is crucial to the narrative: "At my first meeting, I persuaded the board to divide up the names of our 400 subscribers and call each to discuss our commitment to change and to request that they renew their memberships."

As you write your essay drafts, check each sentence to make sure that it includes a key part of the story you are telling. If you can remove a sentence and your essay still makes sense, that line is unnecessary and should remain deleted. However, if your narrative suddenly becomes unclear, that is your proof that the sentence in question is not superfluous and that you are on your way to creating a profoundly connected narrative.

Rule 5: Embrace the Conflict

Although in life, conflict is not typically considered a welcome thing, including conflict in your application essays is actually very important. However, we mean conflict in the *literary* sense, not in the physical or emotional sense (no one wants to hear about you hotheadedly instigating repeated confrontations). In literary terms, conflict occurs when an oppositional force helps shape the story. So, a narrative in which you, as the hero, enjoy a smooth ride toward victory will not be as interesting or exciting as a story in which you suffer some bumps and bruises along the way. For example, most people would find the story of a rookie runner beating an experienced marathoner at the finish line significantly more compelling than the story of an experienced marathoner beating all his fellow runners by a wide margin, never experiencing any competition. The former scenario involves a conflict in the form of an unexpected upset, whereas the latter presents a situation with no inherent surprise or suspense.

In the first part of this chapter, we presented an essay about a youth soccer coach who is immediately challenged by the players and their parents and is forced to respond. If he had not stepped up to this challenge and instead had allowed himself to be bullied, he would have no compelling story to tell. The writer/hero's reaction to the situation and the changes he brings about—in his players, their parents and himself—in response are what shape the story and make it interesting. By including a clear conflict—an oppositional force of some kind—in your essay, you will better hold your reader's attention and maintain the narrative's momentum.

Rule 6: Grab Their Attention

Sometimes the most difficult part of writing a strong essay is determining the best way to start it. Even when you have a strong outline in hand, crafting those first few words or phrases can be challenging. To help you over this hurdle, we offer a few strategies for beginning your essays.

Maintaining the Mystery

Many prospective MBAs give far too much away in the opening sentences of their application essays and immediately present the solution to their story's central conflict—which means they lose their reader's interest just as quickly. (Remember, if you lose your reader, you very likely lose your chance for an admissions offer as well.) Consider the following sample introductory sentences:

I joined the board of the BlackJack Theatre Company three weeks after a failed audit and the executive director's (ED's) surprise resignation.

At Snacks International, the title "summer intern" was a license to get coffee.

When Dr. Gibson, the parent of a child on the soccer team I had agreed to coach, handed me his whistle and said, "Good luck with the kids, but more so with the parents," I finally understood the true challenge before me.

These openers are designed to "tease" the reader and naturally compel him or her to continue reading—to unravel the mystery of the failing theatre, the joke of an internship program, the insanity of soccer parents.

In contrast, consider the following examples, which present no mystery at all:

I was very fortunate to have been an active board member as we saved the BlackJack Theatre Company from a very serious scandal.

At Snacks International, I took over a long-ignored internship program and transformed it into a crucial employee pipeline.

When I coached soccer, I faced many unreasonable and overbearing parents and was forced to get tough with them, ultimately winning them over.

These latter examples are clearly less intriguing. As you write the first line of each of your essays, make sure that you open your story in such a way that your reader is curious to find out what will happen next.

Non-Introduction Introduction

The three positive examples in the previous section illustrate what we call the "*non-introduction* introduction" because they do not follow the conventional tenets of formal essay writing. Candidates who go the more traditional route often craft long and uninteresting introductions that do not convey anything important and use up valuable space (word limits for business school admissions essays are typically 500 words or fewer). Thus, you should instead simply launch into the action of your story so that you grab your reader's interest right away and maintain it throughout the rest of your narrative.

Compare this more traditional and slow-developing introduction

For months, I had been trying to find a volunteer activity that would satiate my desire to both have an impact on my community and engage my passion for the arts. After months of interviewing with various nonprofit institutions, including an art gallery and an artist collective, I found the BlackJack The-atre company, just at the right moment. In fact, I joined the board of the theatre company three weeks after a failed audit and the executive director's (ED's) surprise resignation.

with this more direct and attention-grabbing one:

I joined the board of the BlackJack Theatre Company three weeks after a failed audit and the executive director's (ED's) surprise resignation.

By adding two sentences and 60 words to an essay that is just over 200 words long (the essay appears in full at the end of this chapter), the longer introduction bloats the text without adding any real compelling or useful information. Further, it postpones the action, which increases the likelihood that the reader will lose interest and simply stop reading or tune out. Do not hesitate to begin your story in the thick of the action.

Leading with Your Best

Similarly, many candidates feel that they must start their essays by describing the time frame and job position involved in the story they are about to share, but presenting your essay chronologically is not necessary. You do not always have to outline your history to create context for your narrative. For example, consider the following example of an introduction for an essay about a time when the candidate did something unexpected:

I joined GPT Corp. in 2006, right out of college, knowing that I was entering a conservative culture. As a summer intern and then a member of the managerial rotational program, I was expected to listen and learn, taking on projects given to me by others. When I graduated from the rotational program and became a manager of GPT's $15M real estate portfolio, I could finally make my mark.

This introduction offers significant backstory, but the most impressive part of the writer's story—managing a $15M real estate portfolio—is not mentioned until the third sentence. Valuable word count is essentially wasted on presenting the candidate's less relevant and impressive work. In the following example, the writer instead leads with his best:

Before I felt I could legitimately call myself "manager" of GPT Corp.'s $15M real estate portfolio, I believed I needed to personally visit each of our 19 facilities, from Anchorage, Alaska, to Jacksonville, Florida.

This introduction—just one sentence long, rather than three—introduces the reader to the individual's high-level position right away and is therefore much more compelling and effective.

Overrepresenting Your Overrepresentation

Certain individuals—particularly male investment bankers and Indian software engineers—run the risk of being overrepresented in the MBA applicant pool. As a result—with hundreds, if not thousands, of other qualified candidates who may have similar work experience stories to tell—these applicants often struggle with the idea of how to stand out in their essays. They cannot change their past professional choices, of course, but they *can* introduce themselves to the admissions committee in a way that highlights what sets them apart rather than their similarities to others. Consider the following examples:

As an investment banker, I grew accustomed to the long hours, waiting for that final piece of data I needed to finish an important presentation.

Managing a team to code a new software product for EFG Corp., I meticulously checked my work and that of my teammates, knowing that any glitch could ruin us.

In these examples, the candidates mistakenly—and rather blatantly—introduce the reader to the very overrepresentation they do not benefit from showcasing. Many applicants feel they must start their essays by presenting their title, company name and/or core responsibilities, but as we can see here, doing so is unhelpful in making the candidate stand out or in capturing the reader's attention. More likely, such introductory sentences could make the reader pause and think, "Here we go again."

If you are just such an overrepresented candidate, you must consider your introductory lines quite carefully, and strive to engage your reader by describing your actions, rather than your responsibilities. Consider these alternate openers:

At 5:30 p.m., I could rest easy. The deadline for all other offers had passed, and I knew for certain that the shareholders had finally seen the value in our offer.

Managing a diverse, 12-person team, half in Silicon Valley and half in Pakistan, I felt I needed to first establish a unified culture.

In the first example, the banker candidate avoids a drab self-introduction and instead immerses the reader in an unfolding mystery. In the second, the applicant leads with a standout aspect of his job—the software engineer introduces himself not as a "coder" but as a multinational manager. Every candidate—whether truly overrepresented in the MBA candidate pool or not—should explore alternate openings for his or her essay to avoid the possible pitfalls of overrepresentation.

Rule 7: Respect the Word Count

Although we can assure you that no one will toss your application in the trash if your essays exceed the school's stated word limits a little, in general, sticking as closely as possible to these limits is the best plan. Doing so indicates to the admissions committee not only that you pay attention to and can follow directions (which reflects positively on you as a potential student who will be required to follow numerous guidelines throughout the course of the MBA program) but also that you are willing to put in the work required to convey your story effectively within the stated parameters. Also, you show respect for the school as well as for the admissions readers, who must sort through thousands of essays each week. A good rule of thumb is to not surpass the school's requested word count by more than 5%, though, of course, the fewer extra words you include, the better—and minimizing any risk of a negative impression resulting from exceeding the set word count is best.

Rule 8: Answer the Question

This is our most obvious rule yet, but one that must be stated nonetheless: make sure that you answer the question the school is asking. Sometimes candidates possess a great story and really want to "spin" it for a particular essay prompt. Other times, applicants work and rework an essay so much that when they are done, they do not realize that they have changed their initial story entirely and the resulting essay no longer addresses the school's question. Not answering the question is one of the admissions committees' biggest peeves. In addition to indicating an ability to follow directions on your part (if not an outright attempt to withhold information), not answering the question asked means that you have not provided the information the admissions committee is specifically seeking and needs. So, regularly revisit the essay prompts as you revise your essays, ensuring that you are on track and providing a topical response.

Sample Essays

As you read through our sample essays—the two that appear earlier in Part I of this chapter and the five that follow—please reference the eight rules we have outlined. You will notice that these principles are incorporated throughout.

1. Please describe a time when you coached, trained or mentored a person or group. (500 words or fewer)

At Snacks International (SI), the title "summer intern" was a license to get coffee. How did I know? I had held the position myself and actually counted the number of cups—126—I was asked to fetch while there. When I later joined SI full-time, I asked my supervisor if I could oversee the summer intern program, and he was "delighted to pass it off." Thus, I unceremoniously became intern coordinator.

I met with SI's brand managers and asked each one to complete a simple questionnaire on summer hiring needs. I quickly identified a rather obvious trend—while our seasonal ice cream and sports drink departments could outline multiple summer projects, our hot tea, coffee and prepared soup departments could not define any. So, rather than simply distributing our five summer interns evenly across the five departments that year, I placed them where they were actually needed. After all, training people is difficult when they have no work to do.

I prepared folders for our arriving interns with org charts, employee conduct policies, coupons for leisure activities and descriptions of major summer projects. Then, I met with each individually about their projects, which included researching alternative packaging options and analyzing our advertising spend on certain drinks, to establish deadlines and deliverables.

I let the interns know my door was always open and casually checked in with them at our daily firm-wide meeting. On Friday afternoons, each had a standing appointment with me, and every second Friday, their brand managers joined us for a project update. I had to laugh aloud during my first meeting with Shirley when she remarked that she was doing "real work" while a friend was "just getting coffee for a bond trader."

After four weeks, all our interns were on track with their projects—or so I thought. One afternoon, Christine came to me and said she was unsure of her analysis of our wholesaling alternatives and terrified of presenting her project to our vice presidents. I discovered that she had limited data available and used my relationships to help her source information from wholesalers. I felt with the right numbers in her hands, Christine could handle the analysis. I volunteered to meet with her to focus her study, and her project came together quickly. However, her fear of public speaking was the bigger challenge. I told her if she wanted to "practice, practice, practice," I would be available—always. I listened to Christine present daily during her final two weeks, and we had four practice sessions her final weekend. After her presentation, Christine literally leapt in the air and exclaimed, "I nailed it," which was true: her manager cited her presentation when Christine received her full-time offer.

Christine was not the only one given an offer—all the interns were asked to return, and four accepted. Today, we have eight interns annually, five summer and three winter. Each season, our program grows more robust, and it has become our sole source for recruiting junior staff.

2. Describe what you believe to be your most substantial accomplishment to date, explaining why you view it as such. (200 words)

I joined the board of the BlackJack Theatre Company three weeks after a failed audit and the executive director's (ED's) surprise resignation. At my first meeting, I persuaded the board to divide up our 400 subscribers' names and call each to discuss our commitment to change and request that they *renew their memberships. I was stunned to learn that only 12 subscribers chose not to do so and that 30 donated to the "save the theatre" campaign I had initiated. I then approached area restaurants, which benefit from our 64 performance nights each year, for donations, and applied for a government "nonprofit stabilization grant," quickly raising $34,350—neutralizing much of our debt. After eight hours of debate about a new ED, I prevailed in championing Michael, an entrepreneurially minded playwright who believes in balancing art and finance. His first season, Michael assembled a conservative, crowd-pleasing schedule, and we broke even. Soon, the board asked me to assume the role of president—I accepted. Having had no previous nonprofit experience, I take great pride in having helped save the BlackJack, a 20-year-old civic institution. The worst has now passed. The theater's main drama is back on the stage, where it belongs.*

3. Give us an example of a situation in which you displayed leadership. What did you learn from your experience? (500-word maximum)

Trays of lasagna. Bowls of salad. Trays of freshly cut fruit. When I returned one day from visiting my mother at the hospital, I was surprised to find that our friends had gotten together to make us homemade meals, so that my father, siblings and I could focus on our mother, not on time-consuming but essential tasks like cooking. I could not help thinking, "What if others do not have this kind of support system? Who helps to ease their burden and take care of them?"

Months after my mother's battle with cancer ended, I called the director of St. John's Hospital to propose a program wherein volunteers from one family would assume the costs of and deliver meals to another during a critical family illness. I was surprised by the director's knee-jerk rejection of my idea, citing fairness ("not all families would be served"), privacy issues and—despite my assurances—costs as reasons she was "unenthusiastic" about what I felt was a crucial program.

Frustrated, I went to work addressing her critiques. With respect to fairness, she left me only one choice: expand the program. I had already assembled a list of 25 volunteer families and quickly sent out an email asking them to suggest friends. I created a Twitter feed and a Facebook page where I announced (with permission) each new volunteer family, as did the new volunteers themselves, creating a viral effect. In three days, I signed up 30 more volunteer families, all of whom agreed to pay for the food they would prepare. While scanning the list of volunteers, I noticed a prominent lawyer, whom I approached to develop confidentiality agreements on a pro bono basis. I then asked a graphic designer on the list to create a basic Web site where volunteers could enroll in the program, commit to covering the costs involved and sign confidentiality agreements.

When I returned to see the director, I did so not with an idea, but with a functioning program in hand. With my list of enthusiastic chefs, who had signed confidentiality agreements and committed to paying for the meals, in hand, I went through our site with her. "How can I say no?" she said, shaking her head in disbelief. "Let's give it a shot." That weekend, we delivered our first meals and were met with smiles, hugs and tears. Today, we have more than 150 volunteer families, each committed to cooking four times per year, and dozens of families being cared for throughout our city each weekend.

It is immensely gratifying to see this program "live," but I look back and recognize that I may have been blinded by my own idea and thus did not anticipate the challenges involved. Still, calling on my entrepreneurial spirit, I persisted and acted decisively and resourcefully to alleviate each of the director's concerns and set the program up to succeed. In the end, my ability to implement matched the level of my passion, allowing us all to deliver quite meaningfully.

4. Discuss a setback or failure that you have faced and what you learned from it. (500 words)

"To Irene!" I proclaimed, smiling widely and tipping my glass toward our beloved bookkeeper at her retirement celebration. Inside, though, I felt uncertain about her departure. We had hoped she could stay long enough to train her replacement, but after six months of posting ads and reviewing résumés, we had found no one with the proper accounting skills. Without her, we would be shorthanded.

At lunch with my friends Cory and Joe several months later, I was lamenting that my firm was way behind on its books when Joe, an accountant with Deloitte, suddenly revealed that he had just been laid off. Given his experience, I assumed he could easily manage our books and impulsively asked him if he wanted the job—we paid less than Deloitte, but he would have a paycheck while he looked for other work. He accepted and began sifting through our accounting files in early June, promising to finish our missed internal statements by July.

Yet whenever I passed Joe's desk those first two months, I would find him watching the World Cup online. "So, how are those statements coming?" I would prod, and he would reply, "Irene left a huge mess, so it is taking longer than I had hoped"—or with some other excuse. I was becoming concerned, but he always seemed good-natured and calm, so I accepted that he was making progress.

Still, my doubts continued to grow. Joe and I were Facebook friends, and I noticed he was frequently posting about soccer games, commenting on photos and playing Farmville during work hours. I hesitated to confront him with this information, though, thinking our friendship made that unfair somehow. And he was the accounting expert, not I. Perhaps he was *getting caught up and just happened to check Facebook a lot?*

Two days before our agreed-upon deadline, Joe reported that he had made headway with our books but would not be done for another two weeks. Not knowing enough about the project to understand whether this extension was truly necessary, I uneasily agreed, telling him he had until August 31. After hesitating a moment, I added, "But if our books are not done by then, there will be consequences." Joe reassured me that he understood but again blamed the "mess" he had inherited. Unfortunately, come deadline day, he submitted sloppy statements replete with errors. I fired him on the spot.

My primary mistake was neglecting to properly vet and manage an employee because he was a friend. To avoid repeating this, I have implemented several new procedures. For example, our hiring process now involves three mandatory interviews and two reference checks, regardless of who the candidate is. I also no longer fear being "the bad guy" and readily monitor and push employees to deliver appropriately—especially when I encounter repeated excuses. fAlthough crossing paths with Joe now is awkward, I appreciate all that I learned about the perils of mixing business and friendship, and I am a better manager because of it.

5. What is one interesting or fun fact you would want your future Kellogg classmates to know about you? (25 words or fewer)

My band, Hammond Eggplant, once opened for a band that opened for a band that opened for Bon Jovi in 1983. I am the drummer.

CHAPTER 5

PERSONAL STATEMENT

Personal Statement

Virtually all top business schools ask applicants for a personal statement in which candidates discuss their goals and ambitions as they pertain to their MBA degree and, often, to the target school's particular program. As you approach this essay, be sure that you place the appropriate emphasis on the "personal" aspect of what you plan to write, because you will need to take ownership of and truly tell your story in a way that is not only clear and compelling, but also reveals your personality and individuality. You cannot afford to be generic or vague when stating your goals or the reasons you want to attend a certain school. Instead, you must write with purpose and conviction to convince the admissions committee that you have maturity and vision and will see your goals through.

In practically all personal statements, you must discuss your past (work experience), present (need for an MBA and the school's ability to facilitate your academic and professional objectives) and future (career goals) with insight and focus. However, note that we actually recommend a past, future, present sequence for this essay, because in this case, the most logical approach is to first give context and background about yourself, then describe your goals and lastly, explain why you need the particular school's resources to achieve those goals. Convincingly explaining why a school's resources are uniquely suited to helping you attain your goals is much more challenging when you have not yet stated what your goals are.

Past: Context and Work Experience

In recent years, top MBA programs have been de-emphasizing work history to some degree in their personal statements. Most schools' personal statement essay questions used to read a lot like this:

"Discuss your work history. Why do you need an MBA to achieve your goals? Why do you want an MBA from our program?"

Our conversations with numerous admissions officers have revealed that many feel the résumé, recommendations, other essays and interview provide enough information about a candidate's background that a work history is increasingly unnecessary. However, some schools still take a traditional approach in their personal statement questions, such as the University of California Berkeley's Haas School of Business:

- *A) What are your post-MBA short-term and long-term career goals? How have your professional experiences prepared you to achieve these goals? B) How will an MBA from Haas help you achieve these goals? (750 word maximum for A&B)*

Meanwhile, other schools' prompts, such as those that follow, do *not* explicitly ask about your past experiences:

- **Columbia Business School, 2012**: Why are you pursuing an MBA at this point in your career, and how do you plan to achieve your immediate and long-term post-MBA professional goals? (maximum 500 words)

- **Chicago Booth, 2012**: What are your short- and long-term goals, and how will an MBA from Chicago Booth help you reach them? (500 word limit)

- **Dartmouth Tuck, 2012**: Why is an MBA a critical next step toward your short- and long-term career goals? Why is Tuck the best MBA program for you, and what will you uniquely contribute to the community? (500 words recommended)

If a school directly asks you to discuss your "career progress to date," do not take this as an opportunity to offer every accomplishment on your résumé. Some candidates make the mistake of writing about their work experience for 75% of their personal statements, even though they are also submitting a résumé with their application. This wastes precious essay space by repeating facts the admissions committee already has elsewhere. If you are asked about your work history, we recommend limiting your discussion to approximately 40% of the essay length and including brief, but strong, examples of success to represent an accomplished career.

When no explicit request is made for information about your past, you should still include some brief background to make your present and future goals relevant. For example, a statement like "My long-term goal is to become director of marketing for a major league sports franchise" becomes much more reasonable—and the stated goal seems more attainable—when information about the candidate's past experience in sports management is also offered. Context connects the past and the future. With questions like Columbia's and Chicago Booth's, you should limit your career history to 75–125 words of the final essay—just enough so your career goals are clearly plausible and connect to a broader story.

Admissions committees are much more interested in understanding the decisions you have made and the processes through which you have grown than reading a summary of your past work experiences. Indeed, the presentation of your career progress in your essay should show professional milestones and momentum toward your career goals. Rather than being exhaustive, your career history in this context should be a story that leads the reader to understand and admire your stated goals.

If you are a career changer, as many MBA candidates are, your work history may not seem to link as definitively with your stated goals, at least in comparison with that of someone who plans to continue working in the same industry or job function after business school. However, you still need to show growth and accomplishment and to highlight capabilities and knowledge. Emphasize the aspects of your career to date that are most relevant to your goals, either because they have served as good preparation for your new intended career, or because they have given you some transferable skills that will be relevant to that career.

. . . .
ADMISSIONS MYTHS DESTROYED: THE ADMISSIONS COMMITTEE WANTS A "TYPE"

Many MBA candidates believe that each business school has one distinct "type" of applicant that it seeks. In this world of stereotypes, Harvard Business School (HBS) is looking only for leaders, Kellogg is interested only in marketing students, Chicago Booth and Wharton are seeking only finance students and MIT Sloan wants only "eggheads." Of course, these stereotypes—like most stereotypes—are not at all accurate. Chicago Booth wants far more than one-dimensional finance whizzes in its classes, and it provides much more than just finance to its MBA students (including, to the surprise of many, an excellent marketing program). HBS is not a school just for "generals"; among the roughly 900 students in each of its classes, HBS has a wide variety of personalities, including some excellent foot soldiers. If candidates buy in to these misconceptions and adjust (or abandon) their applications or MBA aspirations accordingly, both they and the schools could miss out on some great opportunities. We hope to be able to convince you to eschew the stereotypes…

By way of example, imagine that you have worked in operations at a widget manufacturer for several years. You have profound experience successfully managing and motivating dozens of different types of people, at different levels, in both good economic times and bad. Even though your exposure to finance has been minimal, you erroneously believe that you must be a "finance guy" to get into New York University's Stern School of Business, your preferred program. So you tell your best—yet naturally weak—finance stories in your application, and suddenly you are competing against a large pool of elite finance candidates who have far more impressive stories to share. Despite the strength of your candidacy, by presenting yourself as what you think the school wants rather than honestly touting your actual strengths and accomplishments, you have essentially sabotaged your chances of being accepted. What if you told your unique operations and management stories rather than trying to compete in the school's most overrepresented pool? Odds are you would stand out much stronger and bolster your case instead.

We encourage you to truly be yourself in your application—try to set yourself apart from all the others and refuse to be easily categorized—and this is what will make the admissions committee take notice. Of course, if you are still not convinced, you might consider what Derrick Bolton, assistant dean and director of MBA admissions at the Stanford Graduate School of Business, wrote on the school's admissions site: "Because we want to discover who you are, resist the urge to 'package' yourself in order to come across in a way you think Stanford wants. Such attempts simply blur our understanding of who you are and what you can accomplish. We want to hear your genuine voice throughout the essays that you write, and this is the time to think carefully about your values, your passions, your hopes and dreams."

Kind of makes sense, right?

• •

FUTURE: CAREER GOALS

Again, your career goals should have a logical (if not a professional) connection to your work history. The general idea is quite simple:

past experience + present MBA = future professional goals

Your stated goals need to show very clear direction and purpose. Simply writing, "When I graduate, I want to go into marketing" or "With my MBA, I will enter the field of consulting" without any further clarification simply is not sufficient—you must explain as specifically as possible what you envision yourself doing after business school. What kind of marketing (e.g., consumer products, business to business, etc.)? What knowledge do you have of consulting, and why will you excel? Remember, this is not a statement of dreams, but a statement of purpose, so you need to provide far greater depth. Stating merely that you "want to be a consultant" will reveal that you have not done your homework and do not really understand your field of interest or your possible place within it.

Consider this goal statement, for example:

After graduating from Tuck, I intend to join either the Performance Improvement Group at Bain and Company, specializing in turn-around strategy, or the Operations Group at BCG, focusing on Rigorous Program Improvement.

Although this sentence is out of context, no one who reads it could credibly argue that the writer does not have a clear sense of purpose or knowledge of the consulting field.

SHORT-TERM GOALS

As you develop your short-term goals, you must consider the specific role they will play in preparing you to attain your long-term goals. You should demonstrate why you will excel in your pursuits and, ideally, show insight into why the market might even need you. Consider the following example:

> *Given my background as a wine journalist, I am well aware of the traditional aspects of the wine-making industry and recognize that many vintners are slow to adapt to modern manufacturing and marketing techniques. With my MBA, I will have the specific entrepreneurial and operational skills necessary to develop a small vineyard and nurture it so that it realizes its full potential. I see myself in my first position after earning my MBA as the general manager of an antiquated vineyard in the ABC region, implementing operational efficiencies, accessing capital for growth and marketing a superior product nationally and even internationally.*

In this example, the writer's experience as a wine journalist connects clearly with his future as a general manager at a vineyard. The candidate identifies a specific role to play and even illustrates the logic behind this role, which is essentially "some vineyards desperately need professional management talent." The reader is therefore left with a clear understanding of where this applicant is going, why he will succeed and even why he is needed in this field.

In short, the admissions committee needs to see conviction and passion for a path; no business school that requests a goal statement is going to accept applicants who are unfocused with regard to why they want an MBA. However, conviction does not need to mean rigidity. Spend some time thinking through your goals very carefully. If you are not able to pinpoint an exact choice—or if you can envision more than one feasible route to your goal—offering an alternative (or two) to your short-term goal may be acceptable. (Note, of course, that any substitute path still needs to involve a logical connection from past to present to future.) Consider the following example of offering alternate goals:

> *In the long term, I would like to head a nonprofit organization that focuses on offering career guidance and mentorship to inner city high school students. I see two possible paths for achieving this goal. In the short term, I could work at a nonprofit with a similar mission, such as the Youngest Professionals Organization, working my way up and gaining concrete experience in managing a nonprofit. Or, I could take a slightly different angle, working at Honesty Corporation, which targets its products to inner city youth, to gain a better understanding of that population before moving from the business sector to the nonprofit one.*

Someone reading this statement should clearly see that the applicant is quite serious about his or her long-term goal—so much so that he or she can envision at least two feasible routes toward it. Admissions committees want to understand that you are resolved about your plans for the future and view earning your MBA as a vital step in the right direction. Sometimes, maintaining perspective and offering a second possible path can reinforce that determination.

LONG-TERM GOALS

When proposing your long-term goal to the admissions committee, again keep in mind that you will need to demonstrate a cause and effect relationship between it and your short-term goal. Note also that long-term goals can be less specific than short-term goals—they essentially represent an ideal aspiration. Although specificity is recommended for statements of short-term goals, admissions committees understand that no one can truly predict the future, so your long-term goals almost by necessity need to be less detailed. However, they should still clearly denote an intended and attainable career trajectory, as shown in the following example:

Given my background as a wine journalist, I am well aware of the traditional aspects of the wine-making industry and recognize that many vintners are slow to adapt to modern manufacturing and marketing techniques. With my MBA, I will have the specific entrepreneurial and operational skills necessary to develop a small vineyard and nurture it so that it realizes its full potential. I see myself in my first position after earning my MBA as the general manager of an antiquated vineyard in the ABC region, implementing operational efficiencies, accessing capital for growth and marketing a superior product nationally and even internationally. In the long term, I would build on the success of this endeavor and would source and acquire multiple vineyards in need of modernization. Ultimately, I see my role in the firm as one of a portfolio manager, actively managing several vineyards and making decisions about capital allocation while leveraging operational and marketing efficiencies.

Avoid Unconnected Long- and Short-Term Goals

While your short- and long-term goals can and should be whatever you desire for yourself and may even seem quite disconnected from each other at first glance, this is fine as long as you demonstrate a cause and effect relationship between them. After all, your long-term goals are based on the assumption that your stated short-term goals will be reached; the positions you will hold later in your career will be facilitated by those you hold earlier.

For example, a statement like "In the short term, I want to be in marketing, and in the long term, I want to become a banker" would present a significantly disjointed transition—one that would likely perplex the admissions officer or career services advisor who reads it. The wine journalist candidate we have used for some of our examples could have written that he aspired to ultimately develop a resort around this vineyard or start his own consulting company, through which he could help other struggling vineyards identify and correct operational inefficiencies—this would have been equally logical and believable. His long-term goal only matters insomuch as it makes sense with his short-term goals—it pairs well, in fact! Given that you will be writing about your own personal goals and part of your vision for your career and life, you most likely already know how they connect for you. The key is clearly communicating for the admissions reader how the transition you envision from your earlier role to your later one will play out in your post-MBA years.

Avoid Disingenuous Goal Statements

Rather than expressing their sincere desires, some candidates make up goals they think the admissions committee wants to hear. These applicants tend to believe that the school is seeking only certain types of candidates who plan to pursue specific industries and positions, so they must fit this mold to gain acceptance to the MBA program. Not only is this untrue, but trying to guess what an admissions committee wants to hear and deliver it is also a recipe for failure. The end result is uninformed goals that lack context and sincerity. And considering that all parts of your application package—including your interview with the school, if applicable—should support the same career vision, presenting false goals here can jeopardize your entire candidacy.

Expressing what you truly feel and want to pursue is key. No amount of sophisticated language can make up for a lack of passion. Remember that admissions readers see thousands of essays every year—they are extremely experienced and can easily tell when a candidate is being sincere and when he or she is just trying to say the "right" thing. Besides, writing the truth is not just more effective, it is much easier.

. . . .

ADMISSIONS MYTHS DESTROYED: I HAVE NO MANAGERIAL EXPERIENCE!

You may find it ironic that formal management experience is *not* actually a prerequisite for getting into a top business school, but keep in mind that an MBA education is for those who aspire to become managers and is not necessarily exclusive to those who already are managers. So, if you are concerned that you have not yet had any subordinates to oversee and feel that not having supervised a staff will preclude you from getting into a top MBA program, let us assure you that you are adhering to a myth and should stop worrying. Instead, focus on how you have excelled in the positions you have held and made the most of other kinds of leadership opportunities.

For example, consider the many investment banking analysts who apply to MBA programs each year. Although these analysts are at the bottom of the banks' organizational charts and therefore do not have staffs to manage, they still have demanding jobs and are required to perform at a high level each day to succeed. So, although these individuals cannot share stories about the standout teams they have led, they *can* talk about thriving in an ultracompetitive environment and can reveal their professional excellence via their résumé, essays and recommendations. And second- and third-year analysts can also discuss how they have trained and mentored younger analysts to demonstrate their leadership skills and potential. So, a title and a formally designated staff are not the only elements that can illustrate one's managerial experience and abilities.

If you have not had any opportunities in your workplace to show that you have the interpersonal skills necessary to lead others, you can turn to your community activities for examples or even share instances of personal leadership. The bottom line is that business schools are not exclusively looking for strictly defined managers but for individuals who demonstrate true promise going forward.

• •

PRESENT: WHY OUR MBA?

Perhaps above all else, business schools want to hear very compelling reasons for each candidate's need for their particular program. Even when a school asks the generic question "Why do you need an MBA to reach your goals?", it is in fact also indirectly asking you, "Why do you need your MBA from *our* school?" and "How will you use our resources to achieve your goals?"

A common mistake among applicants when responding to this question is to simply flatter the school: "XYZ School is remarkable because of its wealth of entrepreneurial resources. I am excited to join a community of aggressive innovators." This sentence is entirely generic; the writer has not offered any insight into his or her reasoning or explained why this particular school's resources are key. Instead, infuse your arguments with school-specific information. For example, using Ross as the target school, this same candidate would be much more effective by writing the following:

> I am interested in modernizing the antiquated wine industry but recognize that no rulebook or simple theorem exists for doing so. Thus, I am compelled by Ross's action-based learning approach, and particularly by its Multidisciplinary Action Project (MAP) course. During my seven-weeks on-site—hopefully at an operationally focused

industry leader like Toyota or United Technologies—I expect to face "live" challenges and deliver targeted solutions, with the help of my peers and advisors. I regard the MAP experience as the ideal training ground as I prepare to face a host of hands-on management problems in the inefficient wine industry.

In this example, the individual does not simply compliment the school's positive qualities but explains how Ross's unique characteristics and offerings meet specific needs. Although you may not always be able to pinpoint aspects of a program that are entirely unique to that school, the key is to show a connection between the school's resources and offerings and your individual interests and requirements—to make the association very clear and personal. Doing so will convince the admissions committee that you have done your homework and understand how the full complement of that school's resources come together to create a unique and fitting experience.

As a rule of thumb, if you can answer the following three questions about the school in some detail, you will present yourself as sufficiently knowledgeable:

1. What specific/unique academic programs or classes appeal to you and will help you reach your goals?

2. How will you both contribute to and benefit from the school's nonacademic offerings?

3. What elements of the school's atmosphere, the nature of its students or the general sense you get about the school through visits or conversations with students/alumni make it attractive to you?

The idea is not to generate a list, but rather to develop a well-thought-out argument. This is similar to stating your case to a jury: prove to the admissions committee that by taking advantage of its school's specific programs in your areas of need, you will achieve your goals, and suggest that taking these specific programs is the best (or only) way for you to achieve those goals. Consider the following example, in which the candidate focuses on Columbia's entrepreneurial resources with respect to attaining his stated goals:

One of the most appealing aspects of Columbia for me is that entre-preneurship is not just taught but experienced through a wealth of hands-on resources. Through the Entrepreneurial Sounding Board, I will have a vital avenue for testing my ideas and will gain frank feedback from serial entrepreneurs, which will allow me to refine my ideas and avoid common mistakes. After examining and refining my business plan with this feedback in mind, I would ultimately apply to the Entrepreneurial Greenhouse, which would provide me with an unprecedented opportunity to prepare my business for its launch and for sourcing investments even before I graduate.

Personal Fit

Showing your academic and career fit with a certain program is vitally important, but so is showing your personal fit. If you have visited the school or spoken with some of its alumni, students, professors and/or admissions staff, mentioning these direct personal connections can be quite helpful. Your knowledge of the program will seem more substantial and your interest more sincere. Note how in the following example, the candidate mentions several firsthand experiences with the school:

I was deeply impressed by my visit to Darden. From Professor Rob-ert Conroy's clever explanation of the AOL case in his "Corporate Finance" course to the energy of my student host, Tom Brown, who took me to First Coffee, Conroy's class and finally his learning team meeting, I was amazed at the dynamic energy that permeated the

Grounds, everywhere I went during my visit. I look forward to being a part of such an outgoing yet close-knit community.

YOUR CONTRIBUTION

Often a school will ask applicants to explain what they will bring to the greater MBA program if they are admitted as students. In this case, applicants can refer to such possible contributions as expected participation or leadership in a particular club; past work experiences, which can enrich classroom discussions; an international background, which can bring a global perspective to teams or course work; or even personal characteristics like enthusiasm or humor, which may facilitate bonding between classmates. Be careful to not just present a list of such options, but to truly personalize your proposed involvement in specific student organizations or events and in the school's broader community. Even when a school does not explicitly ask what you can contribute, if space permits, you should still discuss what you could bring to the community, both in class and beyond, if this has not been accomplished implicitly elsewhere in your essay. Here is one example of how to address the topic of contributing to a school:

> *Outside the classroom, I am excited to get involved in the Operations Club, particularly the Six Sigma Challenge, given my interest in innovating within the wine industry. Needless to say, perhaps, I also look forward to joining and taking a leadership role in the Wine Tasting Club, where I could use my connections to vintners in the region to expand the club's touring program and its connections with recruiters.*

WHY NOW?

An important element of personal statement essays that sometimes gets lost in the shuffle is the "why now" aspect. Candidates understandably focus on detailing their career progress to date, outlining their goals and/or conveying why they are interested in a particular MBA program and either forget or forego any explanation of why they are choosing to pursue an MBA at this particular time. If a school specifically asks why you feel now is the right time to earn your MBA, do not gloss over or omit this information. Do not assume that it is not as important as the other elements of your candidacy that you wish to express—the school asked about timing, and an important rule in writing any application essay is *Answer the question*. Be sure to take the time necessary to develop a clear, fitting answer to this portion of the personal statement, when asked.

SAMPLE PERSONAL STATEMENTS

In this section, we offer several samples of complete personal statement essays. Sample essay A is an example of a "classic" personal statement, for which a school asks applicants to discuss their past experience in depth, whereas sample essays B, C and D are examples of "contemporary" personal statements, for which the school does *not* ask for a profound backstory and has significantly reduced the allotted word count. You will see that sample essays A and B involve the same story from the same person, but in essay A, the candidate discusses his past, his plans and Wharton's offerings in tremendous depth, whereas in essay B, he tells much the same story, only more succinctly, with less detail.

A: Describe your career progress to date and your future short-term and long-term career goals. How do you expect a Wharton MBA to help you achieve these goals, and why is now the best time for you to join our program? (1,000 words)

Declining an offer from a Wall Street investment bank after graduating with a degree in economics, I chose a path that stunned my friends and even my family. I returned to San Antonio to join Gimli Furniture—my family's firm. While I admired my father's success in growing this high-end retail business from a single-location store into an eight-location chain, we both acknowledged that the firm needed to be reinvented. I therefore joined as marketing manager to reinvigorate our Marketing Department, which I quickly realized was stuck in the past. In my first three months, I overhauled our Web site and simultaneously launched flash sales—a heresy in the high-end furniture world. We soon saw a surge in online and in-store traffic, as well as a sustained 15% increase in monthly sales.[1]

Building on this success, I approached my father with another unorthodox idea, but one that met our goal of reinvention—expanding outside Texas. He was initially hesitant, because he knew the local market well. He grasped the potential, however, once I developed a formal business plan that identified nearby Arizona as an ideal expansion destination, given the high number of affluent retirees—our primary customer base—who settle there annually.

As I embarked on an adventure to open our new Arizona store, I did not have access to our Texas infrastructure and was essentially operating as a small business person. Whether I was hiring almost 100 staff members, developing a public relations campaign, managing negotiations with the bank for inventory financing or creating a supply chain from scratch, I was exhilarated by the lead-up to our opening. I felt an incredible sense of pride when my father and I cut the ribbon on our Scottsdale store on Labor Day 2007. Since then—and amid a recession, even—Gimli-Arizona has exceeded expectations. Within two years, we opened two more stores; now these three are our highest grossing. My father and I clearly see that Gimli once again has a bold future ahead.

---

1 When discussing a family business, candidates should show that they have made the most of the opportunity and have had an impact of their own on the organization.

This past Thanksgiving, I returned home to San Antonio, and before I even had a bite of turkey, my father started a conversation that would change my life. He told me he was thrilled with our success and wanted me to expand Gimli across the Southwest before he turned the business over to me in a few years—five at most. He had sketched the terms out in a notebook and stated that, in time, he would begin a well-earned retirement and I would become the company's president.[2] After collecting myself, I set only one condition—that I first earn an MBA. I quoted my father to himself: "Whatever you do, do it right." For me, "doing Gimli Furniture right" means earning my MBA—from Wharton. Only with a Wharton MBA, given the school's strengths in entrepreneurship, finance and family business management, will I possess the skills I need to successfully expand Gimli into a regional chain in the short term and into a national chain thereafter.[3]

In my case, studying entrepreneurship will be essential as I continue to transform our organization. At Wharton, I would pursue the Entrepreneurial Management major. Through courses such as "Strategies and Practices of Family-Controlled Companies" and "Legal Issues Facing Entrepreneurs," I will lay the foundation for expanding Gimli nationally. Further, "Building Human Assets in Entrepreneurial Ventures" will enable me to tackle an ongoing challenge we face—attracting and retaining excellent people despite our limited financial resources. Through the Entrepreneur in Residence Program, I will receive feedback from experienced mentors and continue to reconsider Gimli's long-held but possibly antiquated operating principles. Finally, via the Wharton Business Plan Competition, I could test a new concept store targeted at a younger demographic, and could thereby learn about possibilities for my firm while testing my entrepreneurial mettle.[4]

---

2 The candidate does not simply recite the basic information from his résumé but instead creates a narrative that reveals what is unique about his experiences. Remember, you are telling a story about yourself!

3 The writer clearly states why he is pursuing an MBA.

4 Because the word limit for this essay is quite generous (at 1,000 words), the candidate is able to go into tremendous depth about why Wharton is the right choice for him. Here he explains in detail how the school's entrepreneurial offerings will facilitate his goals.

Although I do not intend to proceed into a classic finance-centered career, finance will still be important to my education, because Gimli's expansion will depend on large, complex financial arrangements. Thus, "Real Estate Investments" will help me determine whether Gimli should expand into rented or owned facilities, and "Corporate Valuation" and "The Finance of Buyouts and Acquisitions" will prepare me to seize long-term growth opportunities. I appreciate the rich array of finance-related resources offered via the White Center and am particularly excited that the traditional focus of its annual seminar is on household financial decision making, given that almost all Gimli's furniture is purchased for the home.[5]

Beyond Wharton's broad course offerings, I am also drawn to the school because of the remarkable expertise it has developed with respect to the unique challenges faced by family businesses. Not only would I benefit from family business–oriented courses and from student groups such as the Wharton Family Business Club, I would immerse myself in family business research at the Wharton Global Family Alliance (WGFA). Wharton's foresight in recognizing the important role family firms play in today's business world—and its leadership in establishing the WGFA—immediately made me feel that the Wharton MBA program is uniquely suited to my needs.[6]

Ultimately, however, what draws me to Wharton is the vibrancy and diversity of its community—something I saw for myself when I visited last month. Sitting in on "Statistical Modeling" with Professor Robert Stine was incredible; the sparkle and humor in the classroom discussion turned complex numbers into a simple but profound forecasting lesson. My student guide, Jane Doe, took me on a campus tour, and I could not get over how she enthused about Wharton—as did, quite literally, the dozens of people I spoke to with Jane. The students I met in Huntsman Hall were friendly and energetic, but most of

---

5 Again, with the greater allowed word count, the candidate can go into great detail—in this case, explaining his need for certain financial skills and naming the specific resources at Wharton that would help him fulfill that need.

6 In this paragraph, the candidate enumerates Wharton's unique programs related to family business, again showing that he has fully researched the school and that his interest is serious!

all passionate about their studies, their future and their Wharton experience. That is what I want out of an MBA program. I want to be passionate about my studies, my future career at Gimli Furniture and my overall MBA experience — and Wharton, more than anywhere else, will bring out that passion.[7]

B: How will a Wharton MBA help you achieve your professional objectives? (400 words)

My friends were stunned when I passed up a Wall Street offer to join my family's furniture retailing business in San Antonio. Since starting as the company's marketing director, revamping our Web site and introducing flash sales to a high-end market that had resisted them, I have taken on a business development role and expanded Gimli into Arizona. In three years, I have opened and led three thriving locations, amid a recession that has forced many others to close.[8] Now, with our firm stronger than ever, my father is preparing to retire and hand the keys over to me. I aspire to lead our firm into new states (New Mexico, Nevada) and new retail concepts (bathware, lighting warehouses), ultimately creating a national footprint. I am in this business for the long haul, and before I take over for my father as president of Gimli, I need to prepare myself for an ever-changing and intensely competitive retail landscape. I need a Wharton MBA.

Studying entrepreneurship via Wharton's Entrepreneurial Management major will be essential as I continue transforming our organization. Courses such as "Strategies and Practices of Family-Controlled Companies," "Building Human Assets in Entrepreneurial Ventures" and "Legal Issues Facing Entrepreneurs" will equip me to expand Gimli nationally.[9] Through the Wharton Business Plan Competition and the Entrepreneur in Residence Program, I will test my ideas for our "warehouse" concept stores and develop a business

---

7   By sharing the story of his campus visit and his interactions with members of the Wharton community, the candidate demonstrates here that he is not only an academic fit with the school but also a personality fit.

8   Though the detail in this introductory paragraph is comparatively less than in the previous sample essay, very little information is lost, and the candidate's situation is still easily understood.

9   Similarly, the level of detail the candidate provides about the school is still rich. Although the total amount of information the writer is able to include is lessened, he still proves that he knows the school's resources well and understands why he wants to attend Wharton.

plan to implement later. In addition, I will dialogue with fellow students in the Wharton Family Business Club who are also managing the complex issues inherent in family transitions.

I also see my need for a profound financial education. "Real Estate Investments" will help me determine whether to rent or own the massive facilities we require; "Corporate Valuation" and "The Finance of Buyouts and Acquisitions" will prepare me to seize long-term growth opportunities. My course work and experiential opportunities will be all the more meaningful because of Wharton's vibrant and diverse community, which I experienced when I visited Professor Philip Stine's "Statistical Modeling Class" last month.[10] I met students in Huntsman Hall who were truly thriving at Wharton and actively creating their envisioned futures. I have never been a bystander in life and have always sought to engage with the world to uncover new opportunities. Wharton provides the ideal platform from which to strengthen and continue building not only my future, but that of my family's company as well.

C: Why is an MBA a critical next step toward your short- and long-term career goals? Why is Tuck the best MBA program for you, and what will you uniquely contribute to the community? (500 words recommended)

After completing my CPA designation at Ernst and Young's Philadelphia office in 2009, I transitioned from the Audit to the Mergers and Acquisitions Department, focusing on restructuring firms in bankruptcy protection. Soon after, I negotiated the sale of a $50M water-bottling company to a French conglomerate, a deal that saved 250 jobs in a one-industry town. Next, I secured $80M for a metal recycling firm, just in time for the commodities boom. I have found this work intellectually challenging and personally meaningful.[11] Still, I want to achieve more—I want to secure the survival of troubled firms.

---

10 The applicant is also still able to personalize his essay and show that he has truly experienced the school firsthand, in this case through a class visit and other on-campus interactions with students.

11 If you read the question carefully, you will see that the school is not asking candidates to recount their development over the past several years. Therefore, this applicant does not need to discuss his progress since college. He just needs to provide brief, yet adequate, context.

My long-term goal is therefore to acquire a distressed firm and lead its turnaround by reshaping its operations and strategy. After identifying an ailing industry, I plan to purchase a struggling company, leverage this acquisition's success and consolidate additional firms, ultimately realizing "deep value" for investors, employees and society.[12] To achieve this, after graduating from Tuck, I intend to join either the Performance Improvement Group at Bain and Company, specializing in turnaround strategy, or the Operations Group at BCG, focusing on Rigorous Program Improvement.[13] With three to five years of consulting experience recommending strategic and operational changes for a multitude of "challenged" firms, I would be ideally prepared to identify my own niche turnaround opportunity.

My CPA designation has facilitated specialized financial knowledge, but I also need theoretical and practical exposure to all management disciplines. Tuck stands out because its sole academic focus is the MBA, and the heart of its program is general management. Tuck's core curriculum is especially compelling because of its breadth, but also because of its immediate focus on management decision making via the "Analysis for General Managers" mini-course and the "Leading Organizations" and "Competitive Corporate Strategy" courses.

Moreover, Tuck's practical opportunities uniquely reinforce principles of strategic thinking. Speaking with current student John Doe, I was excited to discover I could work with likeminded professors and peers to shape my First Year Project and Tuck Global Consultancy experience around my turnaround learning objectives. Through these remarkable hands-on projects, I could develop my targeted learning principles in a "live" environment and on the global stage. Furthermore, I would immerse myself in the Cohen Leadership

---

12 The candidate is not required to follow a structure of short-term goals followed by long-term goals, so he chooses to immediately lay out ambitious long-term goals that are directly connected to his previous work with distressed firms. He then follows with his short-term goals.

13 The candidate is not simply saying, "I want to be a generic consultant." He displays considerable focus and a clear understanding of both where he would fit at these firms and how these positions connect with his stated goals.

Program to benefit from consistent feedback from peers, mentors and coaches, with respect to refining my management style.[14]

When I visited this fall, Tuck Connections matched me with fellow CPA Jane Smith, who guided me on a campus tour and invited me to observe her study group. There, I experienced a vibrant discussion on "The Kodak Problem" and could already see opportunities to share my turnaround experience. Moreover, I witnessed a team environment where discussions and jokes spill out of study sessions. Having attended a small college, I know what "living" a community really means. At Tuck, whether I am helping organize the Winter Carnival or Scavenger Hunt or donning my amateur chef's hat for a Small Group Dinner, I will strive to foster the warm, dynamic community that has made a profound impression on me.[15]

D: What are your short- and long-term goals, and how will an MBA from Chicago Booth help you reach them? (500 word limit)

When I first joined FPC Agencies, none of our clients were using Twitter, and that was just two years ago. Today, one client—a leading car manufacturer—has reduced its TV ad spend by 85%, and we will launch its new vehicle exclusively online. And recently, my firm won the advertising account of a Greek yogurt producer, after I suggested embedding its advertising in mobile video games and pursuing product placement in webisodes. Yet, even as we win business and thrill clients, I cannot help contemplating how to push even further—how can we measure a yogurt ad's impact in a video game or webisode? And how can we optimize such a campaign across all media?

I am pursuing my MBA because I want to shift within the advertising industry from creating advertising campaigns to evaluating business success. I want

---

14 The detail in this section clearly indicates that this candidate has done his homework. He delves into the structure of the curriculum, discusses the appeal of the required core and names several Tuck-specific programs in relation to his stated goals. The reader would not doubt his interest.

15 By revealing firsthand experience with the school, the candidate emphasizes his interest and his fit with its MBA program. You must show not only that you will gain the professional training you need while at the school, but also that you will thrive in the community.

to work with clients to identify goals and measure results. Upon graduation, I would aspire to join a leading interactive digital consulting firm, like NuKidz Marketing or Local 8 Consulting, where, as a consultant, I would both define client expectations and manage marketing programs across channels.[16] After several years participating in and ultimately leading teams to harness consumer data and assiduously tweak clients' Web sites and mobile platforms— thus implementing narrowly targeted and effective marketing campaigns—I would seek to strike out on my own. With my creative experience, analytical mind, client management capabilities, extensive network within advertising and Chicago Booth MBA, I will possess the skills and experience necessary to launch a digital agency whose mission will be to always quantify results.[17]

As I began researching business schools, Chicago Booth's marketing program quickly stood out because of its quantitative focus, which speaks directly to my career needs.[18] "Data-Driven Marketing," "Data Mining" and "Integrated Marketing Communications" are but a few of the courses I would take toward a Marketing Management major. Further, I would strive to unify theory and practice via a management lab course with a marketing focus, which will provide extensive hands-on consulting experience with a leading consumer products firm—and will no doubt be crucial to my career transition. In addition, I would complement my academic experience with the marketing mentorship program and "day at" opportunities, expanding my knowledge of client environments and benefitting from other professionals' experiences in the field.

My leadership skills will allow me to thrive in a client-driven position and ultimately launch my own firm. I look forward to kick-starting the self-evaluation process in the core LEAD course and will continue to hone my soft skills—particularly in negotiations—through the Managerial Effectiveness Group and bolster my decision-making abilities through "Network Structures

---

16 This candidate has a very clear sense of where he wants to take his career, citing firms in his target field and revealing knowledge of what the position entails.

17 The applicant clearly shows a direct connection between his short- and long-term goals.

18 Be very careful with stereotypes. Many candidates assume that Chicago Booth is "only" a finance school, but as you can see here, it offers vast resources in marketing as well. This well-informed applicant's demonstration of how well he knows the school's resources will make him stand out.

of Effective Management" and "Strategies and Processes of Negotiation." I am almost constantly in evaluation mode, examining everything from yogurt ad efficacy to MBA options, but after extensive research and a visit to Professor Dave Goldstein's "Art of Medium Maximization" class, I need no more convincing that Chicago Booth stands alone as the ideal choice for me and my career.

CHAPTER 6

RÉSUMÉ

RÉSUMÉ

Imagine that you are trying to find your way around a major city with which you are somewhat—or perhaps even totally—unfamiliar. Let us use New York City as an example. Suddenly, to your relief, someone hands you a map the size of a standard sheet of paper (8½" × 11"), only it has every single street, park, school, city, government building, business and landmark in the area labeled on it. Most likely, this map would be more overwhelming and perplexing than helpful. Rather than a tool that clearly delineates the most important information you need to get where you want to go, you would have a chaotic assortment of too much information, creating more confusion than clarity.

Now imagine instead that someone hands you a map of the city, but only the major thoroughfares and landmarks are shown. You can clearly distinguish the principal avenues and cross streets and a few significant buildings and spaces, such as Central Park, the headquarters of the United Nations, Rockefeller Center and the Empire State Building. If you were a first-time visitor to New York and trying to quickly orient yourself to the city, which map would you want to use? Our guess is that you would choose the second, more sparse—and therefore more practical—map. Although it might not be helpful in leading you into every nook and cranny in the city (though, we must note, neither would the first map), it would certainly provide the basic information necessary to understand New York's layout and to help you navigate your way to your intended destination.

To an outsider, your résumé is a kind of "map" to who you are, and have been, professionally as well as—to a lesser, but still important, extent—personally. This document quickly familiarizes the reader with your career's major highlights (the landmarks) and your unique skills and accomplishments (the streets and tourist attractions).

Unfortunately, when writing a résumé—whether for a business school application, a job application or any other reason—most people try to include every single bit of information about themselves they think might be relevant and end up with a résumé that is nearly impossible to use, like the first map we described. However, a résumé that instead focuses solely on the most significant data points about the individual—like the second map we described—allows readers to quickly identify and comprehend the writer's major achievements and his or her academic, professional and even life story.

As you approach your résumé, really think about what you want the individual reading it to absorb, rather than what you are worried he or she might miss. You will find yourself in a far better position if someone takes the time to read 100% of the information you provide, even if it represents only 50% of the potential content you could glean from your life, rather than 0% of the information, because you have overloaded your résumé with every possible detail.

Try putting yourself in the shoes of an admissions officer who has to sort through thousands of files; these individuals have neither the time nor the desire to hunt for the relevant information in your résumé. Instead, they want you to make their lives easier and their jobs more efficient. They want you to provide that simple map, with all the important landmarks indicated!

And we cannot stress this enough: please (we beg of you!) do not just hand in whatever you have been compiling since you first applied for a job in the tenth grade. Your résumé is not a throwaway, but an important element of your business school application and a valuable opportunity to make a statement about yourself to the admissions committee!

As you strive to make that statement, keep in mind the three most important aspects of constructing your résumé:

1. Managing your space

2. Maintaining a consistent format

3. Crafting compelling bullets

If you can nail these three components, you should be much of the way toward drafting a résumé that the admissions committee can really use. And is that not the point?

. . . .

ADMISSIONS MYTHS DESTROYED: AT LEAST I DO NOT HAVE TO REWORK MY RÉSUMÉ…

Many MBA candidates do not thoroughly consider and revise their résumés for their business school applications, often dismissing this element because an existing version may already exist on their computer and they do not feel that investing the time to do so would be worthwhile. We strongly caution you not to underestimate the value of this document—the admissions committees review applicants' résumés very carefully, in fact, because they offer a concise summary of the candidate's career, major achievements and personal interests. Yet another misguided approach many candidates take is trying to cram *all* of their life experiences into their résumé. Somewhere between the two extremes—stuffing your résumé with information and ignoring it altogether—lies the ideal: a clear, easy-to-scan, action-/results-oriented résumé, one that tells a story that will capture the attention of an admissions officer who has reviewed hundreds of similar files.

As you prepare your résumé, think about your audience and recognize that this document can be a strategic tool to reinforce certain characteristics that are important to you—characteristics that may complement information provided in other parts of your application. For example, if you aspire to a career that is international in nature, you may place more emphasis on your international experience in your résumé. Or, if you come from a field that is not known for its management orientation—you were a teacher who administered a school's $50K student activities budget, for example—you may use your résumé to emphasize disciplines that are important to an MBA admissions audience.

Some candidates are surprised to realize that one page can communicate so much and thus deserves a significant level of attention, but investing some time in this short but crucial document is definitely worth the effort.

• •

MANAGING YOUR SPACE

When mbaMission hosted the second annual Association of Graduate Admissions Consultants conference in New York, a variety of top admissions officers joined a panel to answer questions from a group of 20 consultants. One consultant asked, "Can you just be definitive—how long should an MBA résumé be?" One admissions officer smiled, looked at the others and said, "All together now!" He then waved his arms like a conductor, and the group sang in unison, "One page!"

Clearly, then, your résumé should be only one page long. Moreover, if you insist on submitting a two-page résumé or longer, your reader may have difficulty scanning it and identifying (and remembering) the important facts. However, this does not mean that you should stuff two pages of content onto one page by shrinking your font and broadening your margins to the edges. Instead, you will need to think carefully about how to manage your space. A few tips follow:

- **Drop the mission statement**: Do not include a mission statement at the beginning of your résumé. Your mission in this case is to get into the MBA program to which you are applying, and the admissions committee already knows this, of course! A mission statement will take up precious space that can be used more effectively for other purposes.

- **Do not include your address**: Only your name should appear at the top of your résumé. You do not need to include your address, email address, gender, marital status, etc., because this will all be provided in your application form. As with a mission statement, adding this kind of information will take up precious space that can be used more effectively for other purposes. (If you want to use the résumé later to apply for a job, just add your address back!) If you simply feel too uncomfortable omitting this information, however, make sure that it takes up only *one* line. Your entire address does not need to be listed as it would on an envelope (i.e., taking up three to four lines).

- **Avoid listing basic computer skills**: The admissions committee will assume that you are proficient in Microsoft Word or PowerPoint and the like. You do not need to list these most basic computer skills in your application résumé—again, such unnecessary information takes space away from more important facts you can include instead.

- **Preserve white space**: You should have ample white space on your résumé so that your reader does not feel overwhelmed by information when scanning your "map." Adjusting the width of your margins can help with this, but you must not make them too narrow and have words practically touching the edges. We recommend no smaller than three-quarter inch margins. Further, you should not make your font smaller than 10 to 12 points, but to balance this, you can minimize the spacing between your lines a bit. No one will notice that this space is eight points high, rather than ten, for example. These kinds of adjustments do require judgment, so you will need to "eyeball" your résumé for readability once you have tinkered with the margins, font size and/or line spacing.

MAINTAINING A CONSISTENT FORMAT

Consistency is absolutely crucial in any résumé. Returning to our map analogy, note that on maps, capital cities are often starred, and the names of large cities are bolded. Without your even realizing it, your eyes are therefore naturally drawn to certain places on the map and this in turn makes the map much easier to use. By using bolding, bulleting, margins/spacing and font sizes consistently throughout your résumé, you likewise help your reader navigate the information you have included.

Although we consider these tips obvious, we feel they are still important to mention: you cannot have random bolding or underlining in your résumé; you cannot switch fonts within a section from one entry to another; you cannot have punctuation at the end of some bullets but not others. Once you decide on the style for an entry or heading, you must maintain that style precisely down the line for all other equal entries and headings. Otherwise, your "map" can become very confusing.

CRAFTING COMPELLING BULLET POINTS

We start this section with a sample bullet point that illustrates much of what you should *not* do when crafting your résumé:

- Responsible for the development of new TV ads for Y-Trade and Dave's Sporting Goods, Internet ads for DSG and Orange Computers and for managing a team of three CEs to advance company objectives in the Internet and TV space.

A total of six things are wrong with this simple bullet—that is *six* mistakes in just 39 words!

1) ***Too long***: As a rule, your bullet points should be brief—no more than two lines each. No one will consistently read bullet points that are three or four lines or longer. If you have trouble shortening a bullet point to less than three lines, odds are that you are trying to discuss too many different aspects of your position, so your bullet point is not specific enough. Work to find where and how you can split the bullet point into two, shorter bullet points. As for our sample bullet point, the individual is trying to showcase multiple types of ads for multiple companies while also trying to discuss his management responsibilities.

2) ***Too many acronyms/jargon***: You may have figured out that the DSG in the sample bullet point is an acronym for Dave's Sporting Goods—though maybe you did not. What about "CEs"? Did you know that this person's firm employs tiers of copy editors and that some are referred to as simply CEs? Of course not! Do not use any abbreviations, acronyms or jargon that are specific to your firm and your industry, and do not assume that your reader will be able to puzzle out abbreviations for things you have mentioned earlier in your résumé. Your reader will end up confused, and your data points will essentially lose their effectiveness.

3) **Focuses on responsibilities**: The bullet point informs us that this person was *responsible for* developing new TV ads, but do we know that any ads were actually developed or that he definitely took part in that development? No! In your bullet points, you must show not that you were *expected* to do something in your position, but that you actually *fulfilled* that expectation. Consider this alternate wording instead:

•   Led the development of new TV ads for Y-Trade and Dave's Sporting Goods…

This bullet point shows that rather than just having been responsible for this task, the individual actually took action and managed the development of content.

4) **Starts with passive language**: Every single bullet point in your résumé should start with a verb, such as *led, crafted, managed, promoted, designed*, etc. Avoid using the same verb over and over again (see Appendix B for a list of hundreds of action verbs you could use), but by starting each bullet point with one, you will demonstrate that you are indeed a "doer" while also incorporating a level of variety into your résumé that will help hold your reader's attention. However, note that not all verbs are *action* verbs. The phrase "Helped team develop ads" may start with a verb, but the action involved is not clear. The reader needs to clearly understand exactly what you have done, so choose your verbs carefully.

5) **Lacks details**: Your bullet points should serve as focused representations of what you have achieved, reflecting well on you and making a solid overall impression. You should never put your reader in a position of having to make assumptions to determine and understand what you have done. Consider our sample bullet point from earlier—did the individual lead the development of ten ads for Y-Trade? Just one ad? We have no idea. "Responsible

for the development of new TV ads for Y-Trade" lacks sufficient data to help us understand. A more detailed, and therefore effective, approach would be as follows, for example:

- Led the budgeting for and production of five TV ads for Y-Trade…

6) ***Does not show results***: As we noted in the third item in this list, the writer explains only that he was responsible for developing ads, whereas he needs to clearly state that he actually did so. Almost more importantly, though, he should offer some evidence to his having been successful in doing so. Were the ads good? Were they produced on time? On or under budget? In your bullet points, you must follow every single action verb and action with a very clear—and ideally quantifiable—result that validates that action. Let us take a look at a bullet point that both describes an action and explains the results of that action:

- Led the budgeting for and production of five TV ads for Y-Trade, completing campaign 10% under budget and two weeks ahead of schedule

This bullet point includes none of our "don'ts" and all of our "dos." You may be thinking, "But not all of my accomplishments are quantifiable. What do I do then?" That is a fair question. If your achievements cannot be measured quantitatively, you can focus on qualitative results instead. Consider the following variations, none of which include a numerically expressible outcome:

- Led the budgeting for and production of five TV ads for Y-Trade, earning follow-on print media projects from client

- Led the budgeting for and production of five TV ads for Y-Trade, inspiring a high commendation from the client

- Led the budgeting for and production of five TV ads for Y-Trade; campaign cited as "excellent" in year-end review

Basically, any action that you have taken that is worthy of being showcased on your résumé should have a result that you can showcase as well. If you have no positive results, why mention it?

If you will allow us to geek it up for a moment, here are these six points expressed as a kind of equation:

Action Verb + Narrow but Detailed Action + Subsequent Result – Abbreviations/Acronyms + Jargon = Powerful Two-Line Bullet Point

Now, let us revisit that original sample bullet point and reimagine the information into a few bullet points that follow our equation:

- Led the budgeting for and production of five TV ads for Y-Trade, earning follow-on print media projects from client

- Created the "Where's Dave?" contest for Dave's Sporting Goods, generating 70,000 hits and 1,000 new customer accounts

- Recruited and managed a team of three copy editors, two of whom received client commendations and were promoted ahead of schedule

We have one final bit of advice about bullet points: do not overuse them. You should not have five bullet points for your current position and five bullet points for a two-month summer internship from six years ago. Carefully consider the "weighting" of your résumé, allowing more bullet points for your current and very recent roles and far fewer for those you have had in the past. For example, you might use five or six bullet points for your current position (assuming you have not just transitioned into it), but anything more simply will not be read by time-pressed admissions officers. We recommend using three to four bullet points for positions in your recent past and one or two for positions held many years ago, as a general rule.

CONSTRUCTING YOUR RÉSUMÉ

As we delve into the writing of your broader résumé rather than just the individual bullet points, we should start by discussing the order of your headings, and therefore of the various sections of your résumé. Typically, your résumé will include the following headings/sections in the following sequence:

- Professional Experience
- Education
- Personal

The admissions officers at the leading business schools are naturally most interested in your professional experience. Thus, you should almost always lead with your professional section (unless you have just earned a PhD or some other similar exception).

Other aspects of your life in which you may have significant achievements and for which you might therefore include sections—so the admissions committee will notice and pay close attention—are as follows:

- Community Work/Leadership Experience
- Military Experience
- Entrepreneurial Experience (outside of traditional work)

We recommend that you limit the number of headings in your résumé to avoid making it too cluttered and causing confusion. For example, if you somehow found time to work, launch a start-up and play a significant role in your community, we recommend that you avoid having five headings in your résumé (professional, entrepreneurial, community, academic and personal). Instead, to streamline your information, you could combine your community and personal sections, so that you just have four headings. The bottom line here is to always use your judgment.

Professional Experience Section

Each major entry in your professional experience section should include the name of your employer, the city and state in which you worked (or city and country if you worked internationally), your job title and the dates of your employment. You might use bolding or capital letters to emphasize your position or firm, but remember, whatever you choose to do, you must present all equal items consistently throughout your résumé (i.e., if your position title for one company is italicized, all your other position titles must also be italicized; if you abbreviate state names in one entry, you must abbreviate them in all others; etc.). Here are two straightforward examples of structures you might use:

PROFESSIONAL EXPERIENCE

XYZ TECHNOLOGIES, Inc.   Tokyo, Japan
Business Development Manager   2010–Present

PROFESSIONAL EXPERIENCE

XYZ Technologies, Inc.   Tokyo, Japan
Business Development Manager   2010–Present

If a company for which you worked is not well known to the general public, you may add a very brief (one line) description of what the company is and/or does. For any organization that is a household name, this is unnecessary, but a company like XYZ Technologies might require a short explanation. Your well-constructed bullet points would then follow.

PROFESSIONAL EXPERIENCE

XYZ Technologies, Inc.   Tokyo, Japan
Business Development Manager   2010–Present

XYZ is a 17-employee, venture-funded, video software start-up.

- Established software-bundling relationships with Moonvideo and Audio4, resulting in $100K in new revenue, which represented 30% of total firm revenue in 2011.
- Managed group of six Web developers and three graphic designers in New York City and Tokyo, completing specialized product launch on time and under budget.
- Lobbied management and obtained budget to attend industry trade show in Las Vegas, acquiring first three advertisers on firm's video platform.

Many candidates mistakenly choose to list only their most recent position with their firm and lump all their accomplishments under this final role, even those achieved in previous positions with the company. Unfortunately, such an approach deprives the reader of the visual cues that reveal promotions. Consider the differences between the two following simplified examples. In the first, the reader is given no indication that the MBA candidate has earned a promotion while with the firm. In the second, the individual's growth is quite clear, and the accomplishments make more sense in context.

Example A:

Mercury Manufacturing   Detroit, MI
Manager, International Purchasing   2009–Present

Mercury is a $430M manufacturing company, specializing in automotive parts.

- Managed seven-person staff to troubleshoot internal supply-chain inefficiencies, reducing costs by 17%
- Determined supplier qualification criteria, training all purchasing staff members to accept/reject supplier bids and determine "preferred supplier" status
- Conducted due diligence on 15 potential suppliers; presented "green light" recommendations to senior management on seven firms, all of which were accepted
- Led team overhaul of shipping and receiving department, leading to reduced paperwork and just-in-time delivery of key product to largest customer
- Established $500 "cost-detective" award program, resulting in 15 employee cost-saving suggestions and $238K in savings
- Sourced inexpensive robotic arm and conveyor belt, convincing Japanese firm to provide free on-site instruction to staff to reduce training expenses

Example B:

Mercury Manufacturing   Detroit, MI
Manager, International Purchasing   2010–Present

Mercury is a $430M manufacturing company, specializing in automotive parts.

- Managed seven-person staff to troubleshoot internal supply-chain inefficiencies, reducing costs by 17%
- Determined supplier qualification criteria, training all purchasing staff members to accept/reject supplier bids and determine "preferred supplier" status
- Established $500 "cost-detective" award program, resulting in 15 employee cost-saving suggestions and $238K in savings

Purchasing Analyst   2009–Present

- Conducted due diligence on 15 potential suppliers; presented "green light" recommendations to senior management on seven firms, all of which were accepted
- Led team overhaul of shipping and receiving department, leading to reduced paperwork and just-in-time delivery of key product to largest customer
- Sourced inexpensive robotic arm and conveyor belt, convincing Japanese firm to provide free on-site instruction to staff to reduce training expenses

As you can see, when we break the experience at Mercury Manufacturing down into two positions, the information becomes easier to scan and "digest," and the individual's promotion stands out.

Perhaps surprisingly, you do not necessarily have to list every professional position you have held thus far in your career. Some positions that are six or seven years old may not offer any useful or currently relevant information about you, and they may not add to your profile (e.g., indicating that you worked in marketing for six months in 2005 may not be useful if you then spent the next four years in consulting). Some candidates with more professional experience may want to consider omitting internships and/ or other quasi-professional experiences in some instances. However, omitting a potential résumé entry requires judgment! Proceed with common sense and prudence.

CONSULTING AND INVESTMENT BANKING RÉSUMÉS

If you have worked as a consultant or in any other kind of environment or role that centers on project work, you can list bullet points that reveal accomplishments and then highlight your most important professional undertakings under a subheading like "Representative transactions," "Selected Transaction Experience" or "Representative project work includes the following." If you are not comfortable including the names of your clients (or are not authorized to do so), simply provide a short description of the client instead, like "$125M Germany-based machine tool manufacturer."

PJ Morton New York, NY

Financial Analyst, Investment Banking Division 2010–2012

- Performed extensive financial modeling and valuation analysis for Fortune 500 companies, earning highest ratings possible at year-end performance review

Selected Transaction Experience

- Completed $500M debt recapitalization for leading technology firm
- Completed $1.1B initial public offering for abcd.com
- Completed $600M senior notes offering for abcd.com

Your professional experience section should always flow chronologically from your current or most recent role to your oldest. If you have worked on any side projects along the way that have been significant, you should likely list this separately from your professional work. To illustrate, let us assume that the manager of international purchasing we highlighted in an earlier example—and whom we will now refer to as Bruce Miller—has started his own eponymous consulting firm on the side (with permission from his firm, of course). We believe the following way of presenting the entries would be confusing—would you agree?

Mercury Manufacturing Detroit, MI
Manager, International Purchasing 2010–Present

Mercury is a $430M manufacturing company, specializing in automotive parts.

- Managed seven-person staff to troubleshoot internal supply-chain inefficiencies, reducing costs by 17%
- Determined supplier qualification criteria, training all purchasing staff members to accept/reject supplier bids and determine "preferred supplier" status
- Established $500 "cost-detective" award program, resulting in 15 employee cost-saving suggestions and $238K in savings

Bruce Miller Consulting   Detroit, MI
Founder (Providing Supply Chain Solutions for Small Business)
                                                                         2011–Present

- Engaged by local agricultural cooperative to reduce transportation expenses, generated gas savings of $5K per year and eliminated the need for one delivery truck
- Completed overhaul of fast-casual restaurant's operations, reducing kitchen waste by 15% and improving average seatings from 3.5 per night to 3.9 per night

Mercury Manufacturing   Detroit, MI
Purchasing Analyst   2009–Present

- Conducted due diligence on 15 potential suppliers; presented "green light" recommendations to senior management on seven firms, all of which were accepted
- Led team overhaul of shipping and receiving department, leading to reduced paperwork and just-in-time delivery of key product to largest customer
- Sourced inexpensive robotic arm and conveyor belt, convincing Japanese firm to provide free on-site instruction to staff to reduce training expenses

Although starting a consulting firm is indeed impressive, listing this accomplishment alongside what Bruce is doing now at Mercury Manufacturing is nonetheless confusing. Instead, Bruce might consider including a separate Entrepreneurial Experience or Consulting Experience section in his résumé, in which he could present his consulting firm work—doing so would help delineate that it is a distinct, part-time experience. (See Bruce's full résumé at the end of this chapter.)

Education Section

Following generally the same format as we have described for the professional experience section, the bare bones of Bruce's education section might look as follows:

EDUCATION

University of Undergraduates	Boise, ID
Bachelor of Science in Business Administration	2010

When composing your education section, consider how long ago you graduated before listing any awards and achievements from your academic career. If you graduated five or more years ago, listing more than three or four bullets under your degree is unwise. One rule that applies to the other sections of your résumé but that you can break in your education section is that you do not necessarily have to show clear actions and results with respect to any leadership positions you held or awards you received. The following would be an entirely acceptable education section for an applicant:

EDUCATION

University of Undergraduates   Boise, ID
Bachelor of Science in Business Administration   2010

- Dean's Award for High Academic Standing – 2008, 2009, 2010
- Thomason Scholarship for top student market research paper – 2009
- Elected Business Administration Representative to the University Senate – 2009, 2010

If you do have clear leadership actions and results you can showcase in this section, however, you certainly may do so, but this is not imperative, as it is in your professional section. The following is another sample education section, this one including information about specific accomplishments.

EDUCATION

University of Undergraduates   Boise, ID
Bachelor of Science in Business Administration   2010

- Managed spring welcome weekend, launching inaugural program and bringing 300 prospective students to campus; resulted in 60% yield compared with 45% for nonparticipants
- Finished second in university's business plan competition, earning a place in the school's venture accelerator
- Elected Business Administration Representative to the University Senate in 2009 and 2010; overhauled student honor trial procedure and gained senate approval for new system

If you are a recent graduate and achieved an incredible amount during your college years, you might consider creating subsections for your awards and activities (if space allows), as follows:

EDUCATION

University of Undergraduates   Boise, ID
Bachelor of Science in Business Administration   2010

Awards

- Dean's Award for High Academic Standing – 2008, 2009, 2010
- Thomason Scholarship for top student market research paper – 2009
- Elected Business Administration Representative to the University Senate – 2009, 2010

Extracurricular Activities

- Managed spring welcome weekend, launching inaugural program and bringing 300 prospective students to campus; resulted in 60% yield compared with 45% for nonparticipants
- Finished second in university's business plan competition, earning a place in the school's venture accelerator
- As Business Administration Representative to the University Senate, overhauled student honor trial procedure and gained senate approval for new system

Community Work/Leadership Experience Section

Some candidates choose to include a separate section in their résumé in which to highlight their leadership activities and/or their community or volunteer work. If you have significant leadership activities tied to notable achievements that you want to showcase—and that will not come across as clearly in a more general (and more brief) personal section—we recommend creating a distinct section for this information, as long as doing so will not detract substantially from the listings in your professional experience section. Showcasing more than one significant community commitment can sometimes be challenging because of space restrictions. Try to limit the number of bullet points for each community commitment to two. A full sample leadership section follows, and the rules we have so far noted regarding formatting, bullets, consistency and so on still apply.

LEADERSHIP

Ye Olde Prep School   New York, NY
Board Member   2010–present

- Established Succession Planning Committee, identifying and hiring new assistant dean to replace existing dean upon his retirement in 2014
- Established Young Alumni Chapter leadership initiative, creating new alumni groups in Los Angeles; Washington, DC; and Boston

Mount Tallman Hospital   New York, NY
Canine Therapy Facilitator   2011–present

- Completed 20-hour training course with Boulder, a 3-year-old Labrador Retriever, and have now conducted more than 50 patient visits together

Personal Section

The personal section of your résumé should not be overlooked or dismissed. This part of the document allows you to demonstrate your personality by highlighting non-work accomplishments, hobbies, special skills and personal passions. This information helps humanize you in the admissions committee's eyes and, in some cases, can even reveal common ground—"You ran the New York City Marathon in 2009? I ran it in 2005!"—which can be especially useful in an interview. Take some time to think about what you have not yet shared with the admissions committee that is an important part of who you are as an individual. This section helps bring what makes you *you* into sharp relief and can thereby add a kind of exclamation point to your résumé. To garner that exclamation point, you must be specific about your interests! Consider the following:

PERSONAL

- Enjoy travel, languages, cooking, reading, music, movies and running

This entry is essentially so nondescript as to be useless and is unquestionably forgettable. Some details are needed!

PERSONAL

- Chinese cooking – have taken three classes at the International Culinary Institute
- Marathons – have completed five marathons in four states
- French Language – participated in three-month immersion in Avignon, France (now fluent)

Although this example omits any mention of the candidate's interest in music, movies and reading, as the previous sample entry did, its narrower and far more detailed focus make the section significantly stronger and more compelling. This individual's best is now more effectively showcased. Although you should always be careful to exercise restraint in this section, listing attention-grabbing interests such as steeplechasing or playing bagpipes (as long as you are truthful!) can really make your interests stand out.

If possible, submit your finalized résumé in your application as a PDF (.pdf). Doing so will ensure that the document will have a much more attractive presentation on screen and also prevents any formatting problems that might otherwise result from printer incompatibility, a mismatch in word processor versions or the use of fonts that are not available on the reader's computer.

We have included several sample résumés on the following pages of this chapter. Because the format of this book involves a smaller page than a standard résumé, much of the formatting will be impossible to convey properly on the following pages. We have therefore created PDFs of these documents so you can view them in their proper one-page format, and these files are accessible in the Resources section of our Web site.

BRUCE MILLER[1]

PROFESSIONAL EXPERIENCE

Mercury Manufacturing   Detroit, MI[2]
Business Development Manager   2010–Present

Mercury is a $430M manufacturing company, specializing in automotive parts.[3]

- Managed seven-person staff to troubleshoot internal supply-chain inefficiencies, reducing costs by 17%
- Determined supplier qualification criteria, training all purchasing staff members to accept/reject supplier bids and determine "preferred supplier" status
- Established $500 "cost-detective" award program, resulting in 15 employee cost-saving suggestions and $238K in savings

Purchasing Analyst[4]   2009–Present

- Conducted due diligence on 15 potential suppliers; presented "green light" recommendations to senior management on seven firms, all of which were accepted
- Led team overhaul of shipping and receiving department, leading to reduced paperwork and just-in-time delivery of key product to largest customer
- Sourced inexpensive robotic arm and conveyor belt, convincing Japanese firm to provide free on-site instruction to staff to reduce training expenses

ENTREPRENURIAL EXPERIENCE

Bruce Miller Consulting[5]   Detroit, MI
Founder, (Providing Supply Chain Solutions for Small Business) 2011–Present

---

1 Notice that Bruce does not include his address. This is entirely acceptable in an MBA application résumé.
2 States are abbreviated in this first entry and are thus abbreviated throughout.
3 Because Mercury is not a household name, Bruce offers a short description of the firm.
4 Bruce breaks up his Mercury entries into two separate positions to better highlight his promotion.
5 Bruce lists his consulting business separately to avoid confusing the reader, who might otherwise wonder whether Mercury or his consulting practice was his main focus.

- Engaged by local agricultural cooperative to reduce transportation expenses, generated gas savings of $5K per year and eliminated the need for one delivery truck
- Completed overhaul of fast-casual restaurant's operations, reducing kitchen waste by 15% and improving average seatings from 3.5 per night to 3.9 per night

EDUCATION

University of Undergraduates   Boise, ID
Bachelor of Science in Business Administration   2010

- Dean's Award for High Academic Standing – 2008, 2009, 2010
- Thomason Scholarship for top student market research paper – 2009
- Elected Business Administration Representative to the University Senate – 2009, 2010

COMMUNITY LEADERSHIP

Ye Olde Prep School   New York, NY
Board Member   2010–present

- Established Succession Planning Committee, identifying and hiring new assistant dean to replace existing dean upon his retirement in 2014
- Established Young Alumni Chapter leadership initiative, creating new alumni groups in Los Angeles; Washington, DC; and Boston

Mount Tallman Hospital   New York, NY
Canine Therapy Facilitator   2011–present

- Completed 20-hour training course with Boulder, a 3-year-old Labrador Retriever, and have now conducted more than 50 patient visits together

PERSONAL

- Chinese cooking – have taken three classes at the International Culinary Institute
- Marathons – have completed five marathons in four states
- French Language – participated in three-month immersion in Avignon, France (now fluent)

John A. Macdonald[6,7]

PROFESSIONAL EXPERIENCE

Flocter & Gramble   Cincinnati, Ohio
Brand Manager   2009–Present

- Initiated $10M television/Internet "Island Vacation" promotion to introduce new Shine brand detergent; surpassed first year's sales targets in three months.
- Mentored and supervised five junior brand managers, each of whom was promoted to brand manager (company traditionally promotes 25%).
- Analyzed daily sales volumes and identified opportunity to increase price point in Midwest, resulting in a 26% margin improvement and $35M in new profits.[8]
- Secured "safe supply" of vital chemical components from alternative suppliers, ensuring 99% order fulfillment.
- Persuaded management to review existing operations; currently leading Manufacturing Review Committee, which will table its final report in June 2013.
- Received "High Performer" award, given to the top 3% of all brand managers, based on sales, profits and a 360-degree review.

XYZ Technologies, Inc.   Chicago, Illinois
Business Development Manager   2007–2009

XYZ is a 17-employee, venture-funded, video software start-up.[9]

- Established software-bundling relationships with Moonvideo and Audio4, resulting in $1M in new revenue, representing 30% of total firm revenue.

---

6 In this résumé, John left justifies his name. This is just a matter of personal preference—stylistic choices of this kind will not sway the admissions committee one way or the other.

7 Only the name is needed here. Notice how the larger font and surrounding white space really make the name stand out. Be careful of using too much emphasis in the document, however, and limit it to your name, position titles, company names and university name.

8 Be as quantitative as possible when listing your accomplishments. Numbers have far greater impact than adjectives. This is especially important with positions of this kind, for which responsibilities can vary widely from one company to the next.

9 Be sure to include a company description if the company is not commonly known.

- Managed group of six Web developers, three graphic designers and three copywriters in New York City and Beijing,[10] completing specialized product launch Web site on time and under budget.
- Created and chaired industry trade group (Independent Video-Software Producers), successfully lobbying for XYZ products as the standard for the market.

FCB Public Relations, Inc.   Tokyo, Japan
Public Relations Intern   Summer 2006

FCB is a boutique public relations firm with offices in Tokyo and Seattle.

- Led Japanese consumer products firm through internal branding development exercises, creating new employee retention strategy.
- Designed surveys and identified more than 400 respondents, completing market research that drove the launch of a new Japanese food product.

EDUCATION

University of ABC   Cleveland, Ohio
Bachelor of Arts – Economics, Honors   2006

- Captain, NCAA Division I Rugby Team, 2002–2006.[11]
- Treasurer, ABC Student Government; managed $200,000 in student funds.
- Publication, *Interest Rate Fluctuations in Canada*, Cambridge Press, 2005.[12]

PERSONAL

- Community: Big Brother, 2008–Present.
- Languages: Swahili (near fluency), French (proficient), Japanese (basic).[13]
- Interests: Play ice hockey three times a week; enjoy Japanese cooking; travelled to 27 countries.

---

10 Whenever possible, list the number and titles of direct reports. Doing so offers insight into how substantial your job is/was. Titles like vice president and director are often given to people who have no reports at all.

11 Athletic accomplishments, especially those that include a leadership role (as this one does), can be helpful, because both admissions committees and employers often see such activities/roles as a reflection of hard work and strong character.

12 Publications, elected positions and awards reflect the high esteem in which others hold you and can often be more impressive in the reader's eyes than self-reported accomplishments.

13 Listing language proficiency not only reveals your range of abilities in this area, but can also reflect positively on your work ethic and character.

Patricia Johnson

EXPERIENCE

Hughes Allan Hamilton   Chicago, Illinois
Manager, Southeast Region Financial Services Group   2011–Present
Representative project work includes the following:[14]

- Top-five publicly traded insurance company – retooled information systems. Analyzed the business and technology strategy and recommended alternative migration strategies, resulting in a 20% cost reduction.
- $15B manufacturer of consumer products – led a team that identified business process improvements for the item processing operations. Completed a detailed cost/benefit analysis that resulted in $5M in annual savings.

Senior Consultant[15]   2008–2011
Representative project work includes the following:

- Top-ten North American commercial bank[16] – compiled business requirements into systems design for a custom investment management system, resulting in a 24% reduction in system costs.
- Top-five privately held insurance company – evaluated business requirements for a universal life system and selected platform systems for acquisition. Migration resulted in closing a redundant 75-person operation center and $11M in annual savings.
- Top-five North American commercial bank – translated business requirements into systems design, resulting in an 11% reduction in the time from application to funding and a substantial increase in capacity

---

14 For banking and consulting resumes, using the "representative project work" or "representative transactions" approach highlights the most substantial accomplishments while leaving the door open to discuss other experiences during an interview.

15 While you may be tempted to leave out earlier titles, be careful. Skillful resume readers know that rapid promotions speak volumes about a person's skills and abilities in a way that self-reported accomplishments do not.

16 To maintain confidentiality, you can "mask" your client engagements. The admissions committees have seen it all and understand such things.

Staff Consultant   2008–2011
Representative project work includes the following:

- Commonwealth Edison[17] – designed and programmed department cost system, implemented on time and on budget.
- Arizona Department of Transportation – designed and programmed a custom revenue tracking system, leading to a 27% decrease in administrative costs in the first year of operation.

EDUCATION

University of QRS   Los Angeles, California
Bachelor of Science, Mathematics; *Magna cum laude.*   2006
- Thesis: "Using Black-Scholes option valuations techniques to model flu outbreaks," published in *Applications Digest*, June 2006.

LEADERSHIP

Head, Anchor Ball Planning Committee
St. Clement Church School.
- Coordinated more than 85 volunteers and set a record for funds raised (over $250,000).[18]

Coach, Lincoln Park High School Soccer
- Organized all events, coordinated transportation and oversaw practices, ultimately leading the team to win the county championship for the first time in school history.

PERSONAL

- Certified Financial Planner, 2009.
- Racing sailboats (finished second in 2008 Mackinac); playing, coaching and refereeing soccer.

---

17 Consider using the actual name of the company for which you consulted if (1) you are comfortable and/or authorized to do so, (2) the name is well known and (3) you think it will make the accomplishments more impressive. Otherwise, a short company description may have a greater impact.

18 Including bullets under a community endeavor can be important in revealing accomplishment in addition to volunteer commitment. Too many MBA candidates list only the minimum information for such activities (organization/date), which means the reader remains unaware of anything of note that the candidate may have achieved.

Matthew Wallace[19]

EXPERIENCE

Grocemania Corporation[20]   Seattle, Washington   2011–Present

Merchandise Planning Manager – Electronics Division

- Led the planning and execution of $1B of annual product distribution and inventory control, achieving $20M in average inventory savings compared with plan.
- Managed and coached 12-person inventory team to negotiate shorter lead times with vendors, resulting in $30M reduction in working capital demands.
- Emphasized team career development; mentored and provided feedback and recognition; as a result, five team members have received promotions.
- Received "Flawless Execution" award, given to top 5% of all division members based on outstanding inventory control and minimized markdowns.
- Led division's 2012 United Way Fundraising Campaign, increasing donations by 7% over previous year.[21]

Buyer – Outdoor Living Division   2008–2011

- Developed creative merchandise assortments and new "exclusive" strategies for $200M division; surpassed sales goal by $25M and surpassed gross margin goal by $7.5M.
- Received April 2010 President's Award (awarded to top 3% of employees firmwide) for leadership in developing and launching an internal generic fertilizer brand. New line generated $14M in incremental sales in 2009.

---

19 Notice the amount of white space here—and the improved readability—created by omitting the candidate's address and goal statement, both of which are unnecessary for an application resume.

20 A small stylistic difference—you will see that Matthew has chosen to put his company name, location and dates of service all on the same line. This is completely acceptable and reflects just a personal preference on the part of the applicant.

21 Although this accomplishment may not be core to the success of Grocemania as a business, it is certainly relevant in that it shows the candidate's diverse abilities and softer personal side.

- Developed cross-functional team of 20 to integrate marketing and finance divisions into category vision and growth; nominated for Collegiality Award.
- Initiated and chaired divisional green committee, reducing paper waste by 50% and division energy bill by 15%.

EDUCATION

State College of Western State   Seattle, Washington
Bachelor of Commerce, Marketing   2008

- Treasurer, Faculty of Commerce Student Body Council, 2003, 2004.
- Student Nominee, Marketing Department Professor Hiring Panel, 2003.

LEADERSHIP & ACTIVITIES

River Heighs Community Center   2010–Present
Youth Sports Leader

- Administered youth baseball league, supervising 10 umpires and 25 coaches across four age-groups.

Special Olympics of Washington   2009–2012
Fundraising Volunteer

- Raised $5,000 in sponsorship fees each year from local businesses.
- Identified and secured a national bronze sponsor, raising $25,000.

PERSONAL

Languages: Spanish (fluent), French (fluent).

Interests: Completed 2012 Boston Marathon, certified Bikram yoga instructor, devoted fan of long-forgotten (and completely awful) B movies.[22]

---

22 Expressing a little flair and humor is acceptable in the Personal section.

CHAPTER 7

LETTERS OF RECOMMENDATION

Letters of Recommendation

Part I: For Candidates

Recommendations play a valuable role in the MBA application process—they provide the only outside information the admissions committee receives about a candidate. In other words, you can largely control the admissions committee's impression of you by what you choose to share in your application and how you present that information, but your control in this area is limited at best. This is why choosing your recommenders wisely and educating them about their responsibilities on your behalf is so important. We have divided this chapter into two parts, the first for you, the applicant, and the second for your recommender (complete with a full sample recommendation). We hope that after reading Part I thoroughly, you will share Part II with those you choose to write your recommendation letters. Many recommenders do not have a clue where to start, so by providing them with some detailed guidance and examples, you can help maximize the impact of these important elements of your application.

Most likely, a few—if not all—of the following questions will instantly spring to mind as you consider your recommendation letters:

- Can I write my own letters of recommendation?

- Who (other than me) should/should not write my letters?

- How can I make sure that the people who write my letters write effective ones?

- How can I make sure the letters get done on time?

Let us tackle these questions one by one…

Can I write my own letters?

The short answer is... No! The long answer is that even though many, often well-meaning, recommenders will offer you that option, writing your own recommendation is not only ethically wrong, but it is also strategically wrong for you. It will deprive the admissions committees of the objective information they need to fully evaluate you. Writing an objective, self-aware, credible letter highlighting your own strengths is almost impossible. And even if you *are* the rare individual who can write intelligently about him- or herself, you still cannot truly see yourself as outsiders do. As a result, you might neglect to discuss traits that the admissions committee would find appealing but that you do not even realize you possess. (Later in this chapter, we will discuss more fully how to manage a situation in which someone asks you to write your own recommendation.)

Who should write my letters?

This may be stating the obvious, but the ideal person to write a recommendation for you is someone who can write a personal and knowledgeable letter that discusses your talents, accomplishments, personality and potential in depth and with an eye toward that which is current. As we will explain later in this chapter, the title of the person writing your recommendation is not all that important. What matters is the substance of the letter that person submits on your behalf.

Current Supervisors/Managers

Most top business schools ask applicants for two recommendations, one of which should come from a current supervisor. For the second recommendation, many MBA candidates typically turn to another professional. After all, who better to discuss your managerial potential than your managers? Some applicants worry that the repetition inherent in this approach will work against them, but that should not be a concern. If you choose two recommenders from the same firm and they both know your work quite well, then they will each have their own perspective from which to discuss your progress and unique experiences to share. So do not be afraid to ask two supervisors.

However, you may not be comfortable asking your supervisor(s) for a recommendation. This is not at all uncommon (we estimate that one out of five applicants struggles with this issue), and in fact, admissions officers regularly advise candidates **not** to request recommendations from their supervisors if doing so could compromise their professional situation in some way. Common reasons candidates may not/cannot obtain a recommendation from a supervisor include the following:

- Candidate has only a brief tenure with the current firm.

- Disclosing business school plans could jeopardize promotions, bonuses or potential salary increases for the candidate.

- Supervisor is "too busy" to help and either refuses the request or tells the applicant to write the recommendation him- or herself, which the applicant is unprepared to do (and, as we have noted, is not advised).

- Supervisor does not believe in the MBA degree and would not be supportive of this path.

- Firm has a policy that managers are not allowed to write recommendations.

- Supervisor is a poor manager and refuses to assist junior staff.

- Candidate is an entrepreneur or works in a family business and thus lacks a credible supervisor

If you cannot approach your current supervisor for a recommendation, consider asking an individual within the same professional realm (or even beyond) who is capable of profoundly and objectively commenting on your performance and skills.

Clients

If you have worked quite closely with a client—maybe you were an external consultant who worked at a client site for an extended period of time, so the client knows your work well—asking this individual for a recommendation could be a very reasonable option for you. A client recommendation can serve as a strong replacement for a supervisor recommendation, if necessary, but it can also be a nice complement to your manager's recommendation by providing a different perspective on your performance.

Past Supervisors

Your recommendation is a window into your current professional performance, so the further back you have to go into your work history to find a potential recommender, the less relevant that person is to you. There is no hard and fast rule about this, but you generally do not want to ask anyone who supervised you more than two years ago for a recommendation. If you recently left a firm to join the one at which you currently work, however, asking two individuals from that previous firm for a recommendation is entirely appropriate, because your newer supervisors may be surprised to learn of your plans to leave (and could respond negatively) and/or may not have adequate fodder from which to draw to craft an effective recommendation. Alternatively, if you are one year (two at most) into a position and had an excellent relationship with a past supervisor who could write a very strong letter on your behalf, you can consider asking that individual for a recommendation. Only you will know if that past supervisor can craft a letter with enough "punch" to warrant such a request.

Counsels/Mentors

If you are your own boss or work in a family business and have been advised closely by a lawyer, business coach or mentor, you might consider asking this individual for a letter of recommendation. As long as he or she can write a letter that is credible—meaning, one that is devoid of empty praise and provides the same objectivity and balance as one from a manager—approaching such an individual is certainly an option.

Community/Nonprofit Directors

If you have been particularly involved in a nonprofit or community activity, and your supervisor in this capacity can speak to your personal and professional attributes, then he or she could provide a recommendation in place of, or in addition to, one from a professional associate. This option requires careful consideration, however—letters from the community service realm generally only work well when the insight into your performance they provide is quasi-professional. You do not need a character reference, but rather a letter that can attest to how you have managed a project, relationship, team, situation or other significant responsibility.

Athletic Coaches/Military Commanders

If a truly formative experience occurred in your life years ago but was in a military or athletic setting, you can consider asking your former commander or coach for a recommendation letter. In such a situation, the individual you approach will have seen you in a highly competitive or stressful situation and can therefore speak knowledgeably about how you responded and what qualities enabled you to do so. Because these kinds of experiences are true "character builders," they allow you to reach into the past for recommendation fodder in a way that others cannot.

WHO SHOULD **NOT** WRITE MY LETTERS?

Your Firm's CEO, a Political Leader or an Impressive Alumnus/Alumna You Met Just Once

Each year, many candidates try to persuade someone with an impressive title or position, but who is largely unfamiliar with their work, to write a recommendation letter on their behalf, mistakenly thinking that the person's stature is more important than what he or she knows and can say. Unfortunately, when this happens, the resulting recommendation is typically vague and ineffectual, because it does not provide the desired personal insight into the candidate—and this undermines the very purpose of the letter. Both the applicant and the recommender will have essentially wasted their time, and the candidate will have missed a valuable opportunity to impress and inform the admissions committee.

Even if you can educate someone far above you in the corporate hierarchy about your achievements to the point where this person can write a more personal letter about you, the admissions reader will likely wonder why and how a CEO, for example, would know what someone so far below him or her in the organization does on a day in, day out basis. So, the authenticity of the letter would come into question and the content would be viewed as suspicious, if not absurd. (If, in fact, your CEO *does* know you and can write a deeply insightful and highly personal letter about your accomplishments and potential, you should not hesitate to approach this person for a recommendation. This is very different from asking a higher-up you met only once.) The same is true for a politician with whom you crossed paths just one time and for any alumnus/alumna with whom you have had only minimal contact. These people cannot be expected to be able to comment knowledgeably about your skills, accomplishments and potential, so any letters they provide would ultimately be unconvincing and ineffective.

Instead of focusing on a person's title or status and relying on it to make an impression on the admissions committee, identify an individual who truly knows you well and can write about your strengths—and even your weaknesses—with sincerity. If your supervisor does not have a spectacular title, this will not reflect badly on you. What will resonate with the admissions office is what he or she says about you and your performance. By being able to share powerful examples of standout achievement that he or she has witnessed firsthand, your supervisor will help you to the fullest.

Professors

Very likely, you are several years into your professional career at this point, and your college professors can really only speak about your past academic accomplishments, rather than your professional achievements and potential. Between your GPA and your GMAT/GRE score(s), the admissions committee will already be able to get a very strong sense of your academic potential, so a recommendation from one of your professors will add very little to your candidacy the way a professional recommendation can. Exceptions are always possible, of course, and a significant one is if you just completed a PhD or your primary work experience has been in a university-affiliated lab—otherwise, you are better served looking elsewhere for a recommendation.

Subordinates

Would you trust that a recommendation letter for a candidate written by someone who depends on that candidate for raises and promotions would be fully honest and objective? No? Neither would an admissions committee. We will not waste any more words on this topic—do not ask a subordinate.

How can I make sure that the people who write my letters write effective ones?

The typical (and misguided) recommendation approach for many MBA applicants is to ask their recommenders to write a letter on their behalf, electronically send these individuals the school's guidelines or form for the recommendation and then sit back and hope for the best. Although this approach could technically work out, it just as well might not. We recommend a much more reliable and effective approach: do some homework before meeting with your recommenders and then sit down with them and set some clear expectations.

Before You Request a Recommendation

For starters, before you approach anyone about writing a letter on your behalf, try to gather some intelligence on your potential recommenders. Have they written letters for anyone else? Are they generous with their time with regard to employee feedback and review sessions? Do you believe they will devote the effort and time necessary to write a letter that will really shine? Are they typically good about meeting deadlines? If applicable, one of the best ways to predict your chances for success with a potential recommender is to research how things worked for any former colleagues who have previously requested a letter of recommendation from this individual. Speak with these colleagues, if at all possible, to find out how the recommender managed the process. By first identifying people who will be helpful and generous in providing a recommendation, you will alleviate the possible stresses of missed deadlines and unpredictable or unhelpful letters.

Meeting with Your Recommenders

Would you believe that business schools actually encourage candidates to meet with their chosen recommenders? Although you may be concerned that doing so might be seen as trying to tamper with the process, nothing could be further from the truth. Top MBA programs want to be sure your recommenders present a full picture of you and recognize that some level of communication and updating on your part is important—if not required—in helping them do so. If you still feel awkward about this step, consider what Derrick Bolton, the Stanford Graduate School of Business's assistant dean and director of MBA admissions, wrote on his blog about recommendations:

> *You should not simply register your recommender and expect her/ him to complete the letter. Sit down with your recommender over coffee, or just in the office, for a few minutes. Explain how important the letter is in the admissions process, and to you. Prepare for that conversation by identifying specific instances that you feel might be helpful for the recommender to highlight. Be prepared to discuss those anecdotes—and to hear the recommender's feedback. To repeat, you should not write the letter of reference, nor should you determine the final content, but I think it's appropriate and helpful for you to talk with your recommender.* [Read the full letter at www.gsb.stanford. edu/mba/admission/dir_references-p.html]

During your meeting with a recommender, you should refresh his or her memory with respect to your accomplishments and progress. Make clear your reasons for pursuing an MBA, your reasons for targeting the schools you have chosen and your ambitions post-graduation. Give your recommenders your résumé and, ideally, a separate list of accomplishments that occurred directly under their supervision (see the sample list we provide at the end of this chapter) so they can easily include key examples of your accomplishments and potential in their letters. Most importantly, impress upon your recommenders the importance of providing real-life evidence of the claims they make about you, wherever possible. (We know from working with some overseas clients that robust, example-filled letters of recommendation are unusual in many countries—if this is the case in your country, do your best to explain to your recommender the importance of full answers laden with examples.)

Keep in mind that, as we explained earlier, you should never write your own recommendation, so go into any meeting with a potential recommender prepared to push back if he or she says, "Just write it yourself, and I will gladly sign it." Most of the time, your recommender will make this kind of offer because he or she believes that allowing you to craft your own letter is somehow doing you a favor, but this is far from the case. Be prepared to tell your recommender that although you appreciate the offer, you would not be able to write as credible, objective or insightful as he or she would and that you are prepared to help with the process in any other way possible. To this end, you can bring with you a "cheat sheet" (see the Sample List of Accomplishments for MBA Recommendation Review Session at the end of this chapter) and a résumé and discuss various applicable anecdotes at great length to help your recommender easily craft an effective letter. The bottom line is that you need this person's participation for the process to work so that you have your best chance of getting into your target school(s).

If you are starting this process early, you can take an important step now and get in touch with former supervisors with whom you have fallen out of contact. You do not want to be in a position where you are calling a former supervisor for the first time in years and asking him or her for a big favor on a tight timeline. If you can identify one whose help you will solicit, reach out to him or her immediately, and then keep the relationship warm over the next few months. You will be far better off when the letter-writing process begins.

HOW CAN I MAKE SURE THE LETTERS GET DONE ON TIME?

One simple and rather reliable way of making sure your recommenders complete their letters by the school's deadline is by giving them extra-early "personal" submission deadlines. This way, if your recommender meets your stated deadline, his or her letter will definitely be available to submit in time for the school's deadline. On the other hand, if one of your recommenders misses your personal deadline, you will still be in good shape, because you will still have some additional time left before the official deadline for this person to complete the letter.

If you are applying to more than one school, your recommenders may have to rework the same letter—or even answer different questions about you—as required by the various applications. You will do both yourself and your recommenders a huge service if, when you initially approach them, you tell them up front that you would like for them to provide a letter of recommendation for each of the schools to which you are applying (i.e., that they will need to prepare more than one such letter, perhaps in more than one format). That way, when you begin working on additional applications, you will not have to go back to your recommender and say, "Oh, by the way, would you mind doing another letter?"

Finally, be sure to actively manage the process throughout. You do not need to contact or visit your recommenders each day and closely monitor their progress, but checking in every few weeks at first and then once a week in the final month or so before the deadline is completely appropriate.

• •

ADMISSIONS MYTHS DESTROYED: MY RECOMMENDER'S GRAMMAR WILL RUIN MY CHANCES

At mbaMission, we are constantly emphasizing effective written communication. Although there is no real "trick" to gaining admission to your target school, earning that coveted letter of acceptance does depend largely on your ability to tell your story in a compelling way in your own words. But how big a role does good grammar play in this process? And if your recommender has bad grammar, will this be detrimental to your chances?

Despite our personal passion for strong written communication, we can assure you that no MBA program will ever reject a candidate because he or she used punctuation incorrectly or broke an accepted rule of style. The admissions committee is seeking to learn about you as an individual and to evaluate you and your potential, both as a student at the school and in your career after graduation. What is most important in your application is that you convey compelling stories that are unique to you—and do so in your own voice. Although you should always strive to perfect your submissions, in the end, the quality and authenticity of your content carry much more weight than your diction and punctuation. And if you are not a native English speaker, you can certainly be forgiven for the occasional idiosyncrasy in your expression.

This is even more true for your recommender. The admissions committee is not evaluating your recommender for a spot in the school's program, so the quality of his or her grammar is largely irrelevant to your candidacy. And the admissions committees can be even more forgiving when English is not your recommender's first language. No school will penalize you for choosing someone who grew up in another country or whose writing skills are not very polished for any other reason. As long as your recommender offers anecdotes about your performance that help illuminate who you are as an individual and that demonstrate that you do indeed possess the abilities and qualities you claim elsewhere in your application, you should be just fine. Substance—not grammar—is always what matters most.

• •

PART II: FOR RECOMMENDERS

Recommendation letters are a vital element of a business school applicant's profile because they offer the admissions committees a truly objective window into the candidate's abilities. For this reason, you, as a recommender, can contribute significantly to your applicant's chances for success, but only if your letter is written in a credible and compelling manner.

MAXIMIZING YOUR IMPACT

To ensure that your recommendation will maximize the candidate's chances of being admitted, you must provide full, descriptive answers to the school's queries and include actual examples of the applicant's accomplishments and potential—this is essential. To that end, we highly recommend that you meet with the candidate to discuss his or her accomplishments (not *responsibilities*, but what this individual has actually achieved and/or brought to pass!). Strive to understand why the applicant was effective and what he or she could have improved in each project or task. Nothing is ethically wrong with discussing these matters together in a meeting—in fact, several top MBA schools encourage such meetings and exchanges of information, because they can help you formulate a clearer picture of the applicant.

When meeting with the candidate, do your best to really understand his or her ambitions, reasons for seeking an MBA and rationale for choosing a particular school. Again, the better you know the applicant and understand his or her approach, the more you will be able to bolster that person's candidacy.

SEIZING EACH OPPORTUNITY

As you write, consider each of the school's questions an opportunity for you to influence the admissions committee. This does not mean discussing every little thing you know about the candidate ad nauseam, however—carefully observe any word limits. Short, powerful statements that reference real-life examples are more valuable than long, wordy answers that are vague or unfocused. At the same time, try to avoid only writing the minimum, and strive to make an impact with each response. For example, your Letter of Recommendation form may request the following: "Please describe your relationship with the candidate, citing how long you have known the candidate and the length of time that you have supervised him/her." In response, you might write, "I am the director of marketing at XYZ Corp., and I have been Jodi's boss for approximately three years."

Although this statement technically fulfills the school's request, the answer does almost nothing to positively support the candidate. It is strictly factual and offers no real endorsement or differentiating value. In contrast, the following response not only establishes the recommender's credibility but also offers details about the candidate's successes:

> *I am the director of marketing for XYZ Corp., but I first met Jodi three years ago, when I was vice president of product sales. At that*

time, I personally hired Jodi as the first member of our New York sales team, and since then, I have seen her professional skills rapidly develop. At first, Jodi leveraged her personality and work ethic to become a leading salesperson nationwide. She truly blossomed as a manager after her promotion to New York sales coordinator and then to vice president of East Coast sales. As I have advanced at XYZ, Jodi has done so in lockstep, so I have witnessed these stages of her career firsthand and therefore feel well qualified to comment on her experiences and potential.

MAKING SUBSTANTIVE CLAIMS

As you write your recommendation, keep in mind that your job as a recommender is not to "sell" the candidate to the admissions committee but rather to present the candidate's true actions and use facts to substantiate your claims, thereby letting the applicant's accomplishments speak for themselves. Real-life examples add credibility to your statements and to your ability to comment on the candidate's achievements.

Superlatives and generalities like "Tom is the most wonderful employee in the world and a great guy!" are actually not helpful, primarily because they are too vague to be useful in making the candidate stand out. However, pairing any superlatives you use with context and "proof" (via examples/experiences) can result in a statement with tremendous value:

Tom's analytical skills are second to none. As a research associate, Tom prepared an insightful and original research note on inflation in Peru that caught the attention of our research director. Soon, as a second-year employee, Tom was de facto promoted to work among a group of our senior economists, many of whom had more than a decade of experience.

Simply stating that Tom's skills are second to none would not have been enough, but following this claim with hard evidence ("insightful and original research," "de facto promotion") reinforces and validates the declaration. This is not selling—this is persuasion. In general, pinpointing two or three of the candidate's strongest attributes and illustrating them with clear and detailed examples should be sufficient.

DIFFERENTIATING THE CANDIDATE

The concept of differentiation is important, because the MBA programs want to accept elite applicants, not just average employees. Thus, any comparison to the candidate's peers is welcome, but the comparison should always place the candidate above others, and this placement must be substantiated by evidence. (Note: We provide more guidance on numerical/quantitative ranking later in this chapter.) Consider the following response to the question "What are the candidate's strengths and weaknesses?":

Bill stands out among his peers because of his extraordinary communication and interpersonal skills. With his confidence, sharp wit and sense of humor, he always captures the audience's imagination at our quarterly conferences, and he is the only one of our six vice presidents to have ever been invited to be a guest speaker at another region's annual sales conference (and has since been asked back twice). Bill is also quite engaging and charismatic on a one-on-one level and has used his personality to motivate others—thereby creating one of our highest performing teams and earning himself two promotions ahead of his peers.

In this case, the reader is told that Bill has some extraordinary skills, and this claim is supported by the revelations that he (1) is the only one to have been invited to a certain event, (2) created one of the company's highest performing teams and (3) was promoted ahead of his peers—three differentiating facts that reveal the candidate to truly be elite.

EVALUATING HONESTLY

Critical feedback—not *negative*, but critical—signals honesty on your part and thereby adds credibility to your recommendation. You may be reluctant to write anything critical, but as long as your comments are constructive (and limited), they can actually add value to your recommendation. However, do not try to portray one of your candidate's strengths as a weakness in an effort to incorporate criticism—this is a peeve of admissions officials: "Suzanne often works too hard. I have pushed her to take more breaks and vacations, but she is just too dedicated." This statement is disingenuous, and the admissions committee will detect this and immediately discount the answer—and possibly your entire letter.

Still, too much honesty is likewise unhelpful. Writing "Suzanne is horribly lazy," for example, would be quite detrimental. If you sincerely feel that your comments about a candidate would be primarily negative or unhelpful to him or her in gaining admission to an MBA program, you should advise the applicant to look elsewhere for a recommendation.

Ideally, you should strike a balance between being honest and not being hurtful, as in the following: "Suzanne is strong as a motivator and can always rouse our team. Still, I think she needs one more 'arrow in her quiver.' I would like to see her exhibit more sensitivity to our employees' needs in one-on-one situations."

FOCUSING ON EXAMPLES, NOT WORD COUNT

No specific length is ideal for a recommendation letter (though it should never exceed any limits the admissions committee has set); your responses just need to be thorough, thoughtful and laden with examples. Often, "less is more." If you try to highlight a dozen strengths your candidate possesses, you will most likely dilute your message to the point that none of the strengths you present will be particularly effective. On the other hand, if you highlight just three strengths and convincingly cite examples to illustrate them, you will have done your job.

The average MBA recommendation might be two or three pages long, but this varies. Substance and depth are more important than length.

RANKING YOUR CANDIDATE NUMERICALLY/ QUANTITATIVELY

Some schools issue recommendation forms that ask you to rank the candidate within a specific percentage range for certain characteristics or skills, such as, "Compared to employees of a similar level, would you say that the candidate is in the top 2% of his/her peers, the top 25% of his/her peers, etc.?" In such cases, the candidate would be best served being ranked highly, of course, yet also fairly and honestly. Consistently claiming that the applicant is among the top percentage across the board will likely not be believable to the admissions committee and could ultimately be less helpful than intended. You should rank your candidate among the top in the areas in which he or she is truly strongest, but for credibility reasons, less high—though still well—in areas where he or she is not quite as accomplished. If you feel that you cannot honestly do this, you may want to discuss this with the candidate before completing your recommendation, because this could notably affect his or her chances of being accepted.

On the following pages, we present a sample list of accomplishments (like one a candidate would provide to his or her recommender) and sample responses (what the recommender would submit to the school).

Sample List of Accomplishments for MBA Recommendation Review Session

Steve Smith, MBA Candidate

John Brown, President, ABC Metal Co. (ABCM)

Background:

- First employee hired via ABCM's on-campus recruiting program

- Hired as assistant purchasing manager, served in this capacity from June 2005 to May 2006

- Promoted ahead of schedule to purchasing manager; served in this capacity from May 2006 to present

- Promotion to vice president (VP) of operations announced; to be confirmed upon departure of current VP in September 2009

Professional Accomplishments:

Assistant Purchasing Manager:

- Managed a $20M widget procurement budget and relationships with 30 suppliers across North America

- Created ABCM's supplier consolidation program, which saved the firm $1.8M in year one

- Initiated ABCM's supplier education program; facilitated three new components, which reduced manual installation and saved 30 man-hours per widget produced

Purchasing Manager:

- Oversaw three assistant purchasing managers and a total budget of $75M; managed relationships with all suppliers (number reduced as a result of consolidation program)

- Applied consolidation program to other two units within firm, generating savings of $5M in other departments

- Mentored three assistant purchasing managers; instituted the ABCM Educational Excellence Program (monthly events continue)

- Initiated and facilitated company hedging program, ensuring predictability of inputs (mixed financial results—saved $500K in copper costs; lost $750K in aluminum)

Vice President of Operations:

- Will join executive team; first nonfamily member to join team

- Will manage the four-member purchasing team and the 40-member manufacturing division

Accomplishments Beyond Professional Responsibilities:

- Started employee recognition program

- Plays on company softball team

Sample Recommendation

1. What is your relationship to, and how long have you known, the applicant? Is this person still employed by your organization (Yes/No)? If "No," when did he/she depart (e.g., August 2010)?[1]

As president of ABC Metals, I represent the second generation of leadership within this family-owned and -managed widget manufacturer. With my son and daughter, who both serve on the executive team, I have been working diligently to cut costs and become more competitive to reinvigorate our firm.[2] It was in this spirit that we decided that we would no longer promote from within, but would institute a college hiring program to ensure that we had "fresh blood."[3] After conducting 20 on-campus interviews[4] for an assistant purchasing manager (APM)[5] at Local State Engineering University, we narrowed our list of candidates to two, and then, after a series of additional interviews and even some psychological and aptitude tests, ultimately chose to hire Steve Smith. As you will learn, this was a turning point for our company. Since Steve joined our firm in June 2005, he has helped energize our company and has earned a promotion to purchasing manager and is patiently waiting to transition into his role as vice president of operations[6] this summer. Because our management team is small, I am able to be a "hands-on" leader and thus know Steve's work quite well.[7]

---

1 You will notice that almost all of the bullet points from the Background section of the applicant's list have been incorporated into this letter.

2 Here the recommender introduces himself, his position and the firm.

3 We feel the need to emphasize that your recommendations will not be checked for grammar or style. Although writing "to ensure that we brought 'fresh blood' into the company" would be clearer, this wording still effectively conveys the recommender's point and will not concern the admissions committee.

4 This reference reveals the depth of the selection process and introduces a comparative element, showing that the MBA candidate has distinguished himself from others.

5 Ideally, any abbreviations your recommender uses in his or her responses should be written out the first time they appear, to avoid any confusion on the part of the admissions reader.

6 Offering such facts proves the candidate's success via promotions.

7 This statement legitimizes the recommender's ability to knowledgeably evaluate the candidate.

2. Provide a short list of adjectives that describe the applicant's strengths.

Entrepreneurial, innovative, intelligent, thoughtful, driven.[8]

3. How does the applicant's performance compare with that of his/her peers?

Steve joined us as an APM and was junior to the other two APM's,[9] who each had seven years of experience with our firm. In fairness, Steve was a college-educated engineer, and our other two APM's did not have similar educational opportunities, but regardless, they were his peers, and he quickly outshone them. In only his third month[10] with the firm, Steve persuaded my son, daughter and me that we needed a revolution in our purchasing program. Rather than spreading our orders to weaken our suppliers' influence over costs, we needed to consolidate and reduce the number of our suppliers to strengthen their dedication to us and eliminate duplication of expenses on our end. Steve's approach saved us $1.8M in our first year,[11] and I quickly promoted him to purchasing manager (PM), unfortunately at the cost of ushering out a veteran manager.[12] As PM, Steve again shone, implementing his consolidation program across all three divisions and saving our firm an additional $5M.[13] Steve was the only PM and thus had no peer in this position; when he assumes the role of vice president of operations this summer, he will replace an individual who is retiring after a 30-year career and will become the first nonfamily

---

8 Keeping this list succinct prevents it from becoming overwhelming, and fewer adjectives are actually more meaningful. The MBA candidate cannot truly be everything, so describing him with too many adjectives can undermine the believability of the list.

9 This is a small issue, but note that the use of the apostrophe here is not correct. This should simply read APMs, because the abbreviation is plural rather than possessive. However, remember that in your recommendations, the admissions committee is worried about content, not grammar, so this kind of minor error will not count against you or your recommender.

10 The recommender immediately offers this anecdote to back up the claim that Steve "outshone" his peers.

11 This fact offers clear and tangible results of Steve's efforts.

12 This sobering note shows that the recommender is not offering only "sunshine."

13 This additional anecdote provides further evidence of the candidate's success and is followed by a comparative element.

member ever to join the executive team.[14] Clearly, Steve has been pro- moted well ahead of schedule at our firm and has excelled beyond any reasonable peer group (new college hires or veteran managers) at our firm.

4. How has the applicant grown during his/her employment with you? Please comment on the applicant's maturity.

In my opinion, it takes a distinctly mature individual to walk into an established family culture and suggest change, all without threatening or alienating others. I have already mentioned Steve's supplier consolidation program, a concept that changed our operations internally as well as our relationship with all of our suppliers. I was profoundly impressed that Steve proactively anticipated the "emotional" effects the consolidation program would have on our remaining suppliers,[15] who might fear being phased out later on, and thus emphasized for them their importance to us by starting the supplier education program. It took tremendous maturity and forward thinking to hold mutual "teach-ins" on a continuous basis at both parties' locations to integrate these suppliers and ensure that we established confidence in them. Since Steve created this program, our re- lationships have never been stronger—we now truly work *with* our suppli- ers, and innovations have actually sprung forth from our closer collabora- tion. Today, Steve represents our firm with our 25 suppliers (down from 70 when he started)—needless to write, a position that requires maturity and judgment, and one in which he has truly excelled.[16]

With respect to growth, I have already noted the promotions that Steve has and will receive and the two programs he has initiated at our firm. Be- yond these quantifiable indicators, Steve's growth can be observed quali- tatively, as he has developed from an individual initiator into an effective

---

14 Again, this recommender can distinguish the candidate as a "first," thereby validating his claim that Steve "outshone" all others.

15 Again, the recommender offers anecdotal evidence to support a claim, in this case maturity. This story demonstrates the individual's level of emotional intelligence.

16 The recommender provides very thorough anecdotal evidence throughout this paragraph and follows with quantifiable facts (e.g., "Steve represents our firm with our 25 suppliers").

manager who develops others' talents. Steve now manages three APM's and does so with a sense of altruism and magnanimity that we all admire. He is always willing to educate others and started our ABCM Educational Excellence Series, leading sessions personally and bringing in guest speakers on Total Quality Management.[17] Steve has transitioned from an individual bubbling with ideas to a leader who, humbly, facilitates discussions, offers his own ideas to be critiqued by others and encourages others to make distinct contributions.

5. Comment on the applicant's ability to work with others, including superiors, peers and subordinates. If the tables were reversed, would you enjoy working for the applicant?

As I just noted, Steve is excited about developing his team and has been an excellent facilitator for it, so much so that he will soon gain responsibility for the 40-member manufacturing team as well. Steve's hallmark is his humility—he treats everyone with courtesy, respect and inclusion, whether he is establishing educational or employee recognition programs or taking his place as the worst player on our company softball team.[18] Steve is constantly thinking of the company and others, recognizing that his growth and the firm's growth depend on a collective. Indeed, he has quite literally broken down the walls in the purchasing department, which has not only saved valuable space, but has also, and more importantly, enhanced communication and promoted a feeling of unity among his team. He no longer has a "privileged" office but is "one of the guys."[19]

If the tables were turned, I would enjoy working for such a magnanimous and altruistic leader.

---

17 The recommender supports his claim about the candidate ("developed from an individual initiator into an effective manager") by relaying an anecdote about the candidate educating others.

18 This humorous jab shows that the recommender knows the candidate well and has genuine affection for him, but is not focused on conveying only positives.

19 Again, anecdotal evidence substantiates the claim that Steve is a team player who is "constantly thinking of the company and others."

6. In what ways could the applicant improve professionally? How does he/she accept constructive criticism?[20]

I think that we were all impressed with Steve's successes with his consolidation program and educational series and simply expected his success to continue. Frankly speaking, his suggestion that we start a hedging program to gain predictability in our copper and aluminum costs was premature. We were not sophisticated enough for these programs, as we did not have the financial expertise to execute them and lost $100K (we were briefly exposed to more than $1M in potential additional costs). I made the final decision to go ahead; after our first six-month term, I cancelled the program and led a reevaluation with my son, daughter and Steve. During this "postmortem," I was clear with Steve that, as much as it seems nonsensical, it can be counterproductive to push the firm too far too fast and that his projections were somewhat naïve, as he had not taken into account a true worst case scenario. It was clear to me that Steve was chagrined and indeed, he went back and reran his numbers, increasing the range of potential crises and quickly determined that the program brought far too many risks to our firm in the near term. We have shelved the program for now, and I am eager to see when he proposes it again, as I am sure that he will only present it when we have grown into it. This will indeed be a test of his patience and development. Regardless, I was impressed by his willingness to accept my criticism and to reconsider his viewpoint.

The fact that he went and reran his models and admitted his errors speaks volumes about him.

---

20 The recommender's answer here is frank and blunt, but it is not damaging. It reveals the recommender as honest and thoughtful, not just a "cheerleader" who refuses to consider the candidate objectively. Although the criticism may "hurt" a little bit, it is not actually harmful to the applicant's candidacy. This is not character assassination, but rather the story of a tough lesson learned.

7. How well has the applicant made use of available opportunities? Consider his/her initiative, curiosity and motivation.

I have offered several examples throughout this letter of initiatives and programs that Steve has undertaken (employee recognition, ABCM Educational Excellence, supplier consolidation and supplier education). His spirit of initiative, curiosity and motivation drive him in a way that I have not seen in my 30 years as president, observing both my own firm and many suppliers and customers. These traits, coupled with humility, are Steve's hallmarks, and they are what make him a uniquely capable individual. In hindsight, Steve was not really given any opportunities and yet he seems to have created so many. When we started our college hiring program, we did not expect that we would hire someone who would become the first nonfamily member of our executive team, and admittedly, it was not because we developed Steve but because we got out of the way and let him go, that this was such a success.[21]

8. Comment on your observations of the applicant's ethical behavior.

When Steve first proposed the supplier consolidation program, it was clear to me that he had considered the effects on all parties. He was not only concerned with dollars and cents, but also clearly understood that we had longstanding relationships with our suppliers and that these would be affected. Further, he was very cognizant that we would become much bigger customers for several small businesses and was concerned about the risks to them. With Steve, I established protocols for dealing with suppliers, including rules stating that we cannot represent more than 15% of a supplier's sales, for fear that it will be too difficult for us to take away business, as too many lives would be dependent on us.[22] We also agreed that we would give any firm at least six months, and preferably one year,

---

21 This is a summary statement, as the recommender has already offered specific evidence. The recommender can make strong statements here because he has already provided evidence that supports them.
22 Again, in this sentence and the next, anecdotal evidence supports the response.

to adjust if we were to remove any business, after implementing our first round of consolidations. I was impressed by the way Steve considered multiple stakeholders and stopped to develop a code of conduct before we implemented—an indication of high ethical values.

9. What do you think motivates the candidate's application to the MBA program? Do you feel the applicant is realistic in his/her professional ambitions?

Because we promoted Steve repeatedly and could see that he was going to be a part of our future, it was imperative that we have open discussions about his potential path.[23] Steve has been determined to pursue an MBA from the start and slowly evolved in his thinking from a part-time MBA to a dedicated two years of study. Even as Steve prepares to join the executive team, we recognize that our firm will have its limitations for him and his growth. In all honesty, the next logical step for him would be to take my position, and I have two family members who are ahead of him in line for the job.[24] Still, we are open to Steve returning and have discussed creating positions for him in the future, maybe even purchasing a smaller manufacturer in a related field for him to manage and integrate.

I recognize that he will go through the recruiting process and that he intends to join a leadership program at a major conglomerate like General Electric or United Technologies.[25] I think that he is entirely realistic in pursuing these positions, and I would enthusiastically endorse him for them, fully aware of the impact he has had at ABCM.

---

23 The recommender reveals here how he would have such intimate information about Steve's long-term plans.
24 This fairly blunt statement again reveals the recommender's honesty.
25 This is another very honest statement and shows that there has been open communication throughout and that Steve sets expectations appropriately.

Steve would benefit immensely from an MBA. He has the engineering and operational skills necessary to succeed, but he needs the financial skills and global exposure to excel once again.[26] I have spoken with him about his MBA plans and am certain that this is a well-timed decision and that he has very carefully considered his educational options, ultimately choosing your program.

10. Are there any other matters you feel we should know about the applicant?

I believe I have covered Steve's various merits in the letter above. Should you have any questions, I am certainly available to answer them.[27]

---

26 It would be unreasonable to expect the recommender to possesses intimate knowledge of the MBA program; thus, he does not go into specifics of what Steve will get out of the program beyond the broader recognition of "financial skills and global exposure."

27 The recommender is under no obligation to add more information at this point if all the important points have already been "hit."

CHAPTER 8

OPTIONAL ESSAYS

OPTIONAL ESSAYS

Our guess is that the vast majority of people reading this book would not recognize the name Greg LeMond, but almost all would know the name Lance Armstrong. Well, in the years before Armstrong "won" the Tour De France (he can no longer be said to have truly won the event), LeMond won it three times. And for a while, LeMond was a celebrity. In fact, he was once *Sports Illustrated* magazine's Sportsman of the Year, when that was a way bigger deal. Today, unless you are a hardcore cycling fan, you probably have no idea who LeMond is, because his remarkable achievements are now well behind him, and he has faded from the spotlight. Armstrong, however, is very much part of our collective conscience, even though his last "win" was in 2005. What keeps him in the public eye is certainly not his cycling achievements, which once seemed quite impressive, but his scandals—his years of denial, his witch-hunts of fellow cyclists and, ultimately, his admissions of guilt. Why do we feel the need to recount all of this for you? We believe Armstrong's story illustrates something important—that scandal sticks with us, and can be damaging, as long as we deny the truth.

We doubt that you have anything of the magnitude of the Lance Armstrong situation in your past—or at least we certainly hope you do not—but if you are considering hiding any element of your candidacy from your target schools, we definitely urge you to disclose it instead. If you, as an MBA candidate, have any issues in your history or profile that would warrant explanation to an admissions committee, follow this golden rule: *Get ahead of the scandal!* Admissions officers, simply put, do not enjoy a mystery. In fact, they hate surprises. They ask applicants for information, and they both want and expect full disclosure. So, disclose.

This is where optional essays come into play in your MBA application process. These essays allow you to explain any aberrations or negative aspects of your candidacy to the admissions committee. Here are a few examples of optional essay prompts from top business schools:

Columbia Business School – An optional fourth essay will allow you to discuss any issues that do not fall within the purview of the required essays.

Duke University's Fuqua School of Business – If you feel there are extenuating circumstances of which the Admissions Committee should be aware, please explain them in an optional essay (e.g., unexplained gaps in work, choice of recommenders, inconsistent or questionable academic performance, or any significant weakness in your application).

Tuck School of Business at Dartmouth College – Please provide any additional insight or information that you have not addressed elsewhere that may be helpful in reviewing your application (e.g., unusual choice of evaluators, weaknesses in academic performance, unexplained job gaps or changes, etc.). Complete this question only if you feel your candidacy is not fully represented by this application.

You will notice that in these prompts, the schools clearly indicate instances in which you *should* write an optional essay. The following are other situations that likely require explanation as well:

- An undergraduate disciplinary issue

- Academic problems/issues

- A nonrepresentative GMAT score

- Lack of a recommendation from a supervisor

- Layoff/firing or significant professional or academic time off

- An arrest, charges and/or conviction

Although the specifics of an issue will vary from candidate to candidate, properly addressing any of these situations requires a certain level of honesty and directness, as we will demonstrate in detail in this chapter. Before we begin, though, we must be clear on two important points: (1) you are *not* required to write any optional essays at all and (2) you should definitely *not* use the optional essay prompt as an opportunity to submit the best essay you wrote for a different school, in hopes that it will score you a few extra points. The optional essay is for briefly discussing a problem—and that is it!

WRITING AN OPTIONAL ESSAY ABOUT AN UNDERGRADUATE DISCIPLINARY ISSUE

Let us begin by offering the example of an individual with whom we worked several years ago—someone with a perfectly valid MBA candidacy but who had a significant blemish on his record. We will call this candidate Ralph.

Ralph had a competitive GPA and GMAT score, both of which were right in the sweet spot for his target schools, and he had been active in his community and worked for what many would regard as a prestige investment firm. He had strong references, a unique personal statement and several other elements in his profile that worked in his favor. Objectively speaking, Ralph was a contender, except—and you were no doubt waiting for that "except"—he had made a big mistake when he was an undergraduate: he had helped a member of his fraternity cheat on a test, and both students were ultimately caught and brought before a disciplinary board. Fortunately, Ralph was smart enough to understand that he should admit his guilt, considering that he was indeed guilty, though he was ultimately suspended from school for a semester.

If you were to meet Ralph, you would probably have a difficult time believing that he could have ever made such a mistake. Maybe he caved to peer pressure from his fraternity brother. Maybe he got caught up in the moment. Maybe he just wanted to help a friend but did so (obviously) in the wrong way. None of this actually matters. Ralph made a mistake, got caught and paid a penalty for his actions. What he likely did not understand at the time, though, is that this mistake would follow him—that he would have a notation on his transcript forever, revealing that he was suspended for a term for academic dishonesty. So when Ralph called us and asked whether he should even bother applying to business school and if so, how he should deal with this issue, we told him we could not *guarantee* that he would get over his "scandal," but we certainly thought it was possible.

To mitigate this blemish on his profile in the eyes of the MBA admissions committees, Ralph needed to write an optional essay acknowledging and explaining the situation. Let us take a look at two sample optional essays on this topic, and then we will analyze and compare them:

During my sophomore year at the University of ABC, I made a naïve and terribly ill-advised choice that has profoundly influenced my academic and personal life ever since. Although I could not see it then, as I look back, the foolishness I exhibited in sharing my take-home exam with a friend is obvious.

When my professor called me into his office one week after the exam date to discuss some "irregularities" he had noted, I took responsibility for my mistake on the spot. After admitting my guilt and making a painful call to my parents, I faced a disciplinary proceeding in which I again took full responsibility for my poor choice in front of a committee of professors and peers. In the end, I was badly humbled and given a three-month academic suspension to think about my poor decision.

After I returned home to Missouri to begin my suspension, it seemed like every week, another of my parents' friends or one of my cousins would come by to visit, and each one would express their surprise at seeing me at home. Over and over, I had to swallow my pride and admit that I had been suspended for academic dishonesty—that I had made a big mistake but accepted the consequences. Although some of my friends got a good chuckle at the situation, and "Boys will be boys" was a regular refrain among my parents' friends, I did not find my circumstances at all amusing. Rather, I found the situation humiliating, though it has fortunately proved life changing. To say that I now fully consider every action and choice before moving forward would be an understatement. Although I am not hesitant to make decisions, I always contemplate their possible ramifications and impact on a very profound level before moving forward.

And here is an alternate approach, by contrast:

When I was in college, I joined a fraternity and thereby agreed to live by a code that decreed I would always help a fraternity brother if asked—no matter what. One day, as I was completing a take-home exam, a fraternity brother who was taking the same course but who almost never attended class, barged into my room and told me to show him what I had written.

My gut reaction was to say no, and initially I resisted, but he was persistent and reminded me of our fraternity pledge to always help a brother in need. Despite my unease, and as more fraternity brothers entered my room and started to harass me, I felt compelled to hand over my exam, just to let him look over my responses. To my horror, he began to copy my work. I protested and kept repeating that we could get in trouble, but he would not listen and continued to copy my work until he had essentially duplicated my exam. I wanted to rewrite my test after that, but I had run out of time and was forced to hand in what I had already written and what had been copied.

When I went to turn in my exam, I should have told my professor about the incident with my fraternity brother and even hesitated outside the professor's office door for a few moments, but I was just too scared about the possible consequences. I was worried that I would be accused of actively cheating, even though my fraternity brother had pressured me into letting him copy my work. (I also worried that my fraternity would consider me a "rat" and ostracize me socially.) In the end, the professor noticed the similarities in our exams, and we were both accused of cheating. Although the other student denied that he had taken part and even accused me of cheating off of him, I admitted my role in the situation and acknowledged to the disciplinary committee that I had indeed made a mistake in sharing my answers. I regret that I helped my "friend" when I clearly should not have done so, and I accepted my punishment in the form of a three-month suspension from school, though I thought the penalty was excessive. I had to return home and live with my parents for several months, which gave me plenty of time to think about how to better withstand such pressures going forward.

Take a moment to consider the differences between these two essays. What characterizes the first example? What characterizes the second? We believe three elements in particular make one of these options much stronger than the other and deserve some closer attention: responsibility, brevity and change.

Responsibility: In the first optional essay, Ralph does not even mention his fraternity or his fraternity brother. Why? Or should we ask, why not? The answer is that Ralph knows that the admissions committee is not interested in reading about his friend or a group to which Ralph belongs. He is writing about himself and his actions and should therefore focus on just his role in the situation. He did not have to share his exam answers with his friend. Ralph was immature at the time of the incident, but he has grown up since—and grown-ups do not shift the blame. Can an admissions officer trust that someone who is trying to place the blame on his friend years later is really a changed man? Can an admissions officer have faith in the integrity of someone who calls his role in this disciplinary issue—one that led to a three-month academic suspension—"minimal"? Of course not. Mature, responsible Ralph (sample essay 1) has a chance of winning over the admissions committee despite this blemish on his record. Immature, irresponsible Ralph (sample essay 2) does not have a prayer. In short, own up to your mistakes.

In addition, as you take responsibility for your actions and decisions, do not be afraid to be brutally honest about your actions. You do not have to mercilessly beat yourself up or go overboard with self-deprecating comments, but honest language helps establish your sincerity and, somewhat ironically, your strength.

To return to Ralph as our example, only if he were an emotionally strong person could he call himself "naïve," his choices "ill-advised" and his subsequent experiences with his family and friends "humiliating." Mature Ralph shows that he can view his situation with the distance necessary to be self-critical. And immature Ralph? Read the second sample optional essay again and try to determine whether immature Ralph uses any language that is honest. The reality is that immature Ralph is focused primarily on making excuses, and in the end, this will not help his cause.

Brevity: You will notice that mature Ralph's piece is just 300 words long while immature Ralph's piece is more than 400 words. Although we cannot recommend a precise word count for all optional essays, given that parameters vary from school to school and also depend on the candidate and the particular situation discussed, keep in mind that shorter is generally better. Mature Ralph's optional essay is better than immature Ralph's for a variety of reasons, one of which is that it makes a more profound statement in fewer words. And we have even seen optional essays that are half this length.

Quite simply, if the issue in question does not require much explanation, then few words may be needed. You should not feel that you need to fill the page! Remember, by the time the admissions officer who reads your application gets to your optional essay, he or she will have already gone through the rest of your application and will likely have read dozens, if not hundreds, of others as well.

So try to put yourself in the admissions officer's position: applications are piling up and you are doing your best to ensure that each applicant gets your full attention, but you have a lot of work ahead of you—and somewhat repetitious work at that. Our point is that by submitting an optional essay, you are essentially asking the admissions officer to do even *more* work. Thus, the key to writing an effective optional essay is to respect this individual's time and be as brief as possible while still conveying all the necessary information.

Change: Whenever you mention a failing of some kind in your optional essay, do your best to reveal that you have changed as a result. Although immature Ralph acknowledged in his optional essay that he regretted the cheating situation and gave the incident plenty of thought during his three-month suspension, he did not discuss how he changed as a result. Mature Ralph, on the other hand, explained that he now has a different, more mature approach to life:

> *Rather, I found the situation humiliating, though it has fortunately proved life changing. To say that I now fully consider every action and choice before moving forward would be an understatement. Although I am not hesitant to make decisions, I always contemplate their possible ramifications and impact on a very profound level before moving forward.*

This is good, but what would be even better is if Ralph could describe some specific actions he took after the incident that would clearly demonstrate that he has separated himself from his past and proactively taken steps to change. For example, if Ralph had returned to school after his suspension and joined the honor committee or the disciplinary committee, or had chosen to enroll in additional ethics courses or perhaps written an essay on his experience for the school paper, he might have been able to include a passage like the following in his optional essay:

> *Rather, I found the situation humiliating, though it has fortunately proved life changing. When I returned to school, I volunteered to write an article about my experience for the school paper entitled "My Best Mistake." Further, I took a "Personal Leadership" course as a prelude to joining the same disciplinary committee that I had had to face. Being accepted to the committee and earning the trust of those who had once sanctioned me was greatly rewarding and symbolized for me that I had been fully welcomed back into my school's academic and social community. To say that I now fully consider every action and choice before moving forward would be an understatement. Although I am not hesitant to make decisions, I always contemplate their possible ramifications and impact on a very profound level before moving forward.*

Of course, if Ralph did not actually take these steps, he could not write about them in his optional essay, but the point is that redemption is important. If you need to write an optional essay, take time first to consider any actions you took to better the situation—or yourself—in the aftermath of the incident, and be sure to include this information in your essay to reveal how you have changed in the interim.

We have spent a lot of words here on Ralph as an example. Why? Ralph had about as bad a blemish on his academic transcript as a candidate could have, short of being expelled or imprisoned. In the end, Ralph's target business schools believed that his error represented a bad blip in his story—but just that, a blip, not a fatal character flaw—and he was admitted to several top-ten MBA programs and even earned a scholarship to one. Clearly, he was able to persuade others that he had changed.

. . . .

ADMISSIONS MYTHS DESTROYED: I DO NOT WANT THEM TO NOTICE MY WEAKNESS!

At mbaMission, we frequently get asked, "If I write the optional essay about my [low GMAT score, low GPA, bad semester in college, long stretch of unemployment], it will call attention to my weakness and overemphasize it, right?" In short, *wrong*. Writing the optional essay about a weakness instead allows you to control the narrative and thereby mitigate the issue.

The admissions committees *will* notice a low GMAT score, low GPA, gap in your résumé, etc.—and if you do not use the optional essay to address the issue, they will be left with unanswered questions about the reasons behind that weakness. Rather than putting the committee in the position of having to guess at an explanation, take control of the situation and grab the opportunity to provide clarifying details. For example, perhaps you have a weak overall GPA because in your first two years of college, you worked full-time, but your GPA from your final two years is much stronger. Not writing the optional essay means that you are hoping the admissions committee will take the time to search through your transcript, note the difference in GPAs, examine your job history to learn that you worked full-time during your first two years and then make the connection between that full-time work and your subsequently lower grades during those years. The odds of this happening are low—admissions officers already have enough on their plates and do not have time to play detective. If, however, you write the optional essay and explain exactly what happened, you no longer have to hope that they will put in that extra effort—you will know for sure that they are evaluating you using complete information. Likewise, you will not have to worry that they will assume an incorrect reason behind your low GPA, because you will have thoroughly outlined the true situation for them.

The bottom line is that admissions officers are professionals whose obligation is to notice all aspects of your profile. Although they are not punitive, they are also not careless and will readily identify weaknesses like those we have mentioned here. At the same time, they are only human and are dealing with thousands of applications. Any way that you can save them effort by clearly guiding them through your story can only work to your advantage.

WRITING AN OPTIONAL ESSAY ABOUT AN ACADEMIC PROBLEM/ISSUE

Just as the admissions committee would expect you to discuss a disciplinary issue, it would also expect to you to address pure academic issues. Although punitive situations are somewhat uncommon, academic issues are not. The most common ones we have encountered with candidates include the following:

- Weak undergraduate GPA (anything less than a 3.0 or converted equivalent)

- Poor semester or year(s), though with a final overall GPA of 3.0

- Failing grades (Recovering from an F or two is not unheard of.)

- Poor performance in quantitative classes (e.g., statistics, calculus) or management classes (e.g., finance, accounting)

- Repeatedly switching majors throughout college

- A relatively low GPA in absolute terms but high in relative terms (e.g., a chemical engineer from India with a 68% overall yet finished at the top of his or her class)

- GPA conversion that requires explanation because it is based on a different scale

If you have one or more of these issues, take a deep breath and know that not everyone who gets into business school had perfect grades in college. Then, address your issue directly, keeping in mind the key points for optional essays that we have presented thus far—accept responsibility, focus on brevity and demonstrate change. Now read the following sample optional essay with these elements in mind:

When I was in college, I was very devoted to extracurricular activities. I was the president of my fraternity and volunteered as a Big Brother, activities that took 20 hours per week. During my freshman year, I was so busy with my fraternity that I had trouble balancing my studies, and I finished the year with a 1.9 GPA. Thereafter, I improved dramatically, and I finished my college career with a 3.3 overall. Clearly, I learned balance with time.

What is wrong with this statement? Primarily, the candidate does not take real responsibility: he uses extracurricular involvements as an excuse for his poor academic performance and displays absolutely no soul-searching or maturity. Many individuals work to put themselves through school or are heavily involved with volunteer activities while in college yet are still able to perform at a high level academically. This person's social schedule did not prevent him from achieving academically—he prevented himself from doing so by choosing instead to spend his time away from his studies!

In contrast, consider this alternate approach:

My first year of college was an adjustment period for me, as anyone can clearly see from my transcript, which shows my 1.9 GPA for the year. For a brief period at the beginning of my freshman year, I mistakenly put my fraternity ahead of my academics, but thereafter, the pendulum swung the other way. Even though I took on more responsibility within my fraternity, I made sure that my classes were always my first priority. From the beginning of my sophomore year, my GPA each semester was never lower than a 3.7, and my cumulative GPA at graduation was a 3.3. I regret that the 19-year-old me left a blemish on my transcript. I feel strongly that the 3.7 GPA I earned for six straight semesters better represents the kind of student I truly am and ask that the admissions committee view me this way.

What works here? First, the candidate takes responsibility: he describes why his overall undergraduate GPA was lower than he felt it should be, but rather than using his membership in a fraternity as an excuse, he explains that at first, he found himself distracted from his studies but was later able to regain his focus. Second, the essay is brief—the writer does not belabor the point unnecessarily and conveys all the relevant information in less than 150 words. Third, he demonstrates change: his steady grades during his final three years at college serve as proof not only of his academic aptitude but also of his altered focus and his subsequently consistent dedication to his classes.

You may be wondering, "What if my grades never improved while I was in school? What if I missed the boat entirely?" If this is the case, you should definitely address the situation in an optional essay, and, as we discussed in Chapter 1, "Fundamentals of an MBA Candidacy," hopefully you can offer some mitigating evidence bolster your story. Consider the following sample essay:

> *Four years have passed since I graduated college with a 2.7 GPA and a degree in biology. In hindsight, even I can see clearly that I lacked the maturity at the time to grasp the opportunities before me. Two years ago, I enrolled in LMNOP University's extension program and have since taken "Calculus I" and "Corporate Finance I," maintaining my focus and earning As in both classes. Although I largely squandered the intellectual opportunity college offered, I am doing my best to make up for lost time. Today, as a twice-promoted brand manager at ABC Corp., I know that I have grown and have identified my professional and intellectual passions. I am looking forward to two years at XYZ Business School, where I intend not only to perform, but also to seize every opportunity to expand my intellectual horizons.*

Why is this essay effective? Again, the writer fulfills the three primary criteria for an effective optional essay: taking responsibility, offering evidence of change and keeping things brief. He takes responsibility for his initial academic shortcomings ("squandered an intellectual opportunity") and then reveals evidence of and his desire to change through his enrolling in additional classes, making strong grades and earning promotions. And he achieves all of this in just six sentences!

You may be questioning whether you really need to disclose such an issue or whether the admissions committees would even notice. The answer to both questions is "Yes!" Admissions officers will not simply look at your overall GPA and assume this tells them everything they need to know about your entire academic history. Instead, they will look for trends and aberrations in your four-year transcript, trying to understand the deeper story behind your individual grades. As a result, they appreciate any additional information that might clarify a seemingly uncharacteristic moment or period in your college career. So, if a mystery lurks in your transcript—such as a 1.9 GPA in your first year of college followed by a 3.7 or higher each year thereafter—be sure that you tell the admissions reader that tale.

Sometimes a poor GPA is a matter not of judgment but of consequence. Life can throw people curveballs, and individuals often have to make the most of a challenging situation. In the following sample optional essay, a candidate with a low GPA explains to the admissions committee the special circumstances behind his academic record:

My parents, neither of whom graduated from high school, never encouraged me to go to college and did not save for my education. I attended JKL University because it offered me a partial scholarship, but I still needed to work 40 hours per week to cover my remaining tuition costs and living expenses.

I take great pride in the fact that I worked two eight-hour shifts at Shmuli's Electronics each weekend as an hourly salesperson, and then worked four hours three days per week as well. During my summers, I worked overtime, often as much as 60 hours per week, so I could take some of the pressure off during my academic year. I am certain that my 3.0 cumulative GPA would have been higher had I worked less and studied more, but that was simply not an option for me, and keeping my Shmuli name tag on my desk motivated me in my studies. Ultimately, I became the first in my family to earn a college degree, and I am proud that I was able to graduate debt free.

This essay is effective because the candidate is not asking the admissions reader to feel sorry for him. In fact, he takes quite the opposite approach, expressing his pride in the sacrifices he made for the sake of his education and revealing how his job motivated him in his course work. In this case, the applicant is certainly brief but clearly takes responsibility for his choices and actions. He does not reveal that he has changed in any way, but he does not actually need to, because his dedication and character are not in question and were obviously strong from the start.

As we noted earlier, sometimes a candidate will have a primarily strong academic track record but his or her transcript includes an irregularity or aberration that is worth explaining. Let us consider the following sample optional essay by an individual whose transcript shows just such an anomaly:

A quick examination of my transcript will reveal a significant aberration during my third year of college. After earning a cumulative GPA of 3.85 during my first two and a half years, I have a series of voluntary withdrawals in the second semester of my junior year. Right before that semester began, my mother was diagnosed with cancer. At her insistence, I returned to school when classes began, but my mind was clearly elsewhere, and I soon withdrew from my courses and re-

turned home. Again, with her encouragement, I returned during the summer semester in hopes of catching up on my course work and being able to graduate on time, but I quickly realized that being home to care for my mother during her treatment was too important to me. We were fortunate to discover that by the end of the summer, her chemotherapy and radiation treatments had worked, and her cancer had gone into remission. I graduated just one semester late with my GPA intact, but more importantly, with my mother's health restored.

Again, this is a straightforward, credible statement of explanation, which is supported by facts. When an applicant who otherwise appears to have been a capable and committed student has this kind of aberration in his or her transcript, the admissions committee will only naturally wonder about the circumstances behind the deviation, so providing clarification via an optional essay is a good idea. Again, the applicant in this case is not asking for pity but is simply explaining her circumstances, and thereby displays a level of maturity admissions committees find appealing.

We can think of almost too many possible circumstances that could affect someone's GPA, including bankruptcies, personal illnesses, originally pursuing the wrong coursework and switching majors, so we cannot address them all here in this chapter. Just remember the basic keys to an effective optional essay—accept responsibility, focus on brevity and demonstrate change—and simply apply them to your specific situation.

The optional essay can also be used to directly address a technical issue related to your academic record. A common such issue is a difference in grading scales between the target business school and the candidate's undergraduate institution. When writing about an issue like this, just stick with presenting the most basic facts and offering an explanation—and then move on. Consider the following simple example:

As requested, I have converted my GPA using your suggested scale, and my 80% overall translates to a B average. Given that my undergraduate institution's records office states on its site that grades of 80% are given to the top 10% of the class and 90% to the top 1%, I feel that your conversion of my 80% to a B average may understate my performance. I cannot provide guidance for what an appropriate conversion of my percentage might be, but I do ask that the admissions committee consider my academic performance with this context in mind.

Why is this essay effective? The writer quickly explains why his grades need special interpretation, but he does not belabor the point, nor does he express anxiety or concern for what the alternate conversion might bring. He simply presents the issue for the admissions committee's review and assumes that the appropriate considerations will be made.

WRITING AN OPTIONAL ESSAY ABOUT A NONREPRESENTATIVE GMAT SCORE

No doubt many business school applicants have wondered whether they should explain or justify their GMAT score to the admissions committee. When might doing so be appropriate?

- When your score is on the low end or even outside the school's GMAT range

- When your overall score is high but your Quantitative score is low

Ideally, in writing an optional essay about your GMAT results, you will be able to declare that you truly do have the skills necessary to succeed in business school and can demonstrate evidence of these skills. Consider the following two sample optional essays, wherein the applicants work to mitigate any concerns the admissions committee might have about their ability to manage MBA course work by offering proof of relevant skills via professional experience, designations earned and grades from past courses:

1) After seeing my score on my first GMAT, I was pleased by my 700 overall but surprised to see a low Quantitative raw score (43). I have long considered my quantitative and analytical abilities strengths, evidenced by my having completed all three levels of the Chartered Financial Analyst exam on the first try and my two years as an investment banker, where I am immersed in analysis each day. I hope that for now, the admissions committee will recognize that my low Quantitative score is an anomaly. I am confident that given my educational and professional experiences, I will be able to effectively manage LMNOP University's challenging MBA curriculum and contribute to my learning team and to classroom conversations.

2) I have taken the GMAT four times, and to my dismay, and clearly not because of a lack of determination, I seem unable to score higher than a 630 overall. Unfortunately, my best scores on each section of the test—a 48 Quantitative raw score and a 39 raw Verbal score— did not occur on the same day, and my scores have fluctuated with each try. I am disappointed to be applying with an overall score that is well under LMNOP University's average. I earned As in accounting, economics and finance as an undergraduate and know that I have the aptitude and intellectual abilities to perform in your MBA program.

Writing an Optional Essay about a Lack of a Recommendation from a Supervisor

As we discussed in Chapter 7, for a candidate to be unable or unwilling to obtain a recommendation from a direct supervisor is not uncommon. As Harvard Business School's managing director of admissions and financial aid, Dee Leopold, explains on her blog, you should not worry that you are disadvantaged if you do not have a current supervisor writing one of your recommendations:

> *Please don't jeopardize your employment in order to secure a recommendation from a current employer. While we might wish that all bosses were enthusiastic and encouraging about business school for their emerging leaders, this is not a universal sentiment. Make your best judgment call about whom to ask, make sure they understand what we're asking, explain your choices to us if you think you should... and that's it!*

As Leopold notes, simply explain why you are not submitting a recommendation from your direct supervisor and then present the reasons behind your alternate selections.

> *I have elected not to inform my supervisor of my desire to pursue an MBA, because I believe doing so may adversely affect my year-end bonus and possibly even my employment. Instead I have asked my former manager, David Stephenson, with whom I worked closely for two years as assistant brand manager (ABM) to his brand manager at ABC Corp., to write a recommendation essay for me. During my time as ABC, I progressed from intern to ABM and thus developed from a researcher to a decision maker. Mr. Stephenson supervised me during this formative part of my career, and I am confident that his opinion is still quite relevant and indeed profound.*

I have also asked Steve Jones, my relationship manager at QRS Ltd.—my firm's most significant client—to share his insights on my performance. I have worked with Mr. Jones on an almost daily basis for eight months, speaking with him about purchasing decisions, and I am the only person from outside his company who attends his monthly planning meetings, where I help manage his purchases. I feel that Mr. Jones knows my professional abilities well and will offer a sincere appraisal of my skills.

This essay is effective because the writer presents a clear, reasonable explanation for the lack of a supervisor's recommendation—without making excuses or requesting a special exemption—and then presents strong reasons his alternate recommenders are amply qualified to assess his abilities and potential. In addition, he does so in less than 200 words.

WRITING AN OPTIONAL ESSAY ABOUT A LAYOFF /FIRING OR SIGNIFICANT PROFESSIONAL OR ACADEMIC TIME OFF

We addressed absences from college earlier in this chapter with our example of the college student who withdrew from courses to attend to her ailing mother, and just as you need to explain any breaks from your undergraduate studies, you should also address any gaps in your résumé. If you have a notable gap in your résumé or academic transcript, understand that this should be explained in an optional essay but that it is not a Scarlet Letter of any kind that will immediately disqualify you from serious consideration by the admissions committee. The schools do not expect each and every applicant to have progressed along a clear and unbroken track to business school from day one of their professional careers and will not dismiss a candidate's application if he or she has taken some time off from work—whether voluntarily or involuntarily. The following three sample essays illustrate various ways applicants might rationalize such an absence. The common attribute among all three is that the writers make no excuses and leave no mysteries, and if you must write an essay on this topic yourself, you should be sure to follow their lead.

1) As a 22-year-old college graduate, I took a chance and declined a job offer from a consulting firm, choosing instead to travel the world. For the next 14 months—essentially until I exhausted myself—I helped run a hostel in Peru to finance my travels in South America, served as an English-speaking tour guide in Prague to extend my travels into Eastern Europe and performed manual labor on a farm in New Zealand to be able to explore the Asia-Pacific region. During this time, I learned enough Spanish to hike four days to Machu Picchu and spend eight days sailing through the Galapagos, all with Spanish tour guides; I milked cows and goats two hours north of Auckland and learned to surf on Australia's Bell's Beach. I also met people from practically every country in the world while I led tours of "Baroque Prague" and later travelled with four of my tour attendees to Red Square and the Hermitage. Needless to write, perhaps, taking those 14 months to see the world was one of the best decisions of my life. I returned home with remarkable memories, experiences and friends around the world, but also with a resolve. I was fortunate to return during a boom time, and the consulting firm again extended me a job offer, which I accepted. I appreciated the company's loyalty and have attempted to pay it back through hard work. Since joining ABC Consulting in the fall of 2009, I have been promoted ahead of schedule and continue to take on more responsibilities. I have satiated my wanderlust for now—though I know travel will always be a part of my life.

2) Like many in the financial community, I never imagined a day when Lehman Brothers would cease to exist. What seemed to me to be the safest position in the world clearly was not, and I found myself laid off from my analyst position in 2008, struggling to break into the financial world as the hiring picture got worse and worse. I took a disciplined approach to my job hunt and sent my résumé to three firms in the financial field each day, but as the crisis intensified, I knew that I was facing long odds of reestablishing myself on Wall Street. In the meantime, I started to volunteer at a local elementary school, teaching math in an after-school program and mentoring budding entrepreneurs through Junior Achievement. I also started to look for small firms outside New York and again, sending out no less than three résumés a day, I remained optimistic. I eventually took a position with George Bros., a small asset management firm in Minneapolis, in the spring of 2009. I have truly enjoyed the opportunity to transition to the buy side of finance, and even though it took 11 months, I feel fortunate to have landed on my feet as the market remains challenging.

3) I was unsure what I wanted to do upon graduation from college and took a sales position with a software reselling firm simply because, quite frankly, it was offered to me through an on-campus interview and I needed the job. I was unsure that this was a wise choice, and within only a few weeks of my start date, it became clear that I was a poor fit with the company. Although I enjoyed the people at Micro-Choices, I was not passionate about the firm's products and services. After six months, I was in the lowest quintile in terms of sales performance and was let go. I knew the decision was not personal—it was a numbers game, and my numbers were poor.

For the next six months, I lived with my parents so that I could reduce my personal overhead and give myself the breathing room to take the right job. I completed dozens of informational interviews and started to focus my efforts on sales in the digital media space. I joined MacroBright after three interviews and two team lunches and have felt comfortable with my role and the company's products from the beginning. I am confident that my job performance—evidenced by my promotion and my supervisor's recommendation—attest to how far I have come and my ability to make smart career choices.

In each of these essays, the applicant follows our basic rules: accepting responsibility, focusing on brevity and demonstrating change. Although we cannot guarantee that writing an optional essay will always allow you to overcome a "scandal" in your profile, adhering to these guidelines will certainly give you your best chance.

WRITING AN OPTIONAL ESSAY ABOUT AN ARREST, CHARGES AND/OR CONVICTION

In the context of an MBA application, an arrest or low-level criminal conviction is embarrassing to disclose but not impossible to overcome. If you have been arrested for underage drinking or even drunk driving, for example, this will probably not disqualify you from getting into an MBA program. We have helped a number of candidates who successfully overcame such indiscretions in their applications. Consider the following sample optional essay by a candidate who had been charged with driving under the influence:

On December 12, 2011, I pleaded "no contest" to the charge of driving while impaired, surrendered my license and agreed to perform 100 hours of community service. I completed those hours in three months, even though the judge had mandated a six-month time frame, volunteering with Mothers Against Drunk Driving (MADD). I continue to work with MADD to this day, speaking to school groups about my experience and helping in the local chapter's office, stuffing envelopes and performing data entry.

The Sunday I was charged, I had made the most serious error in judgment of my life by driving home after watching football at a friend's house and ingesting a number of beers. In doing so, I put not only my life—but more importantly, the lives of others—at risk. I made an awful mistake that day, but I have definitely changed, and I am doing my best to make sure that others do not make the same error in judgment that I did.

Why is this optional essay effective? The writer is clearly contrite and offers no histrionics. He is brief in his statement but still gets his point across. And finally, he presents evidence of his penitence, which is then reinforced by considerable proof of change, indicated by his continued volunteer work. Any balanced reader should accept the writer's statement and recognize that he has matured and that this incident should in no way prevent him from being a successful business school student or professional.

CHAPTER 9

INTERVIEWS

INTERVIEWS

The MBA interview can take on a variety of forms. Some business schools allow for applicant-initiated interviews and offer candidates the opportunity to schedule an interview at their leisure, while other interviews are school initiated, meaning the admissions office will extend an interview invitation only to selected applicants after reading their applications. Some schools even employ a hybrid model, wherein before the application deadline for a round, candidates can request and complete an interview. After the deadline, however, interviews are by invitation only.

The person who conducts your interview can vary from program to program. Some admissions offices conduct all candidate interviews themselves either on campus or in hub cities across the United States and foreign countries, while others will ask students or alumni to interview applicants in person or even over the phone. (Recently, some schools have even experimented with Skype.)

Another differentiator is that at some schools, interviews are "comprehensive," meaning that your interviewer will have read your entire application cover to cover at least once before your meeting, whereas at others, your interview will be "blind," meaning that your interviewer will have seen only your résumé and thus will not know your GMAT score or GPA (unless, of course, this information is on your résumé), or the content of your essays.

Regardless of the venue, the person interviewing you and whether your interview is blind or comprehensive, your goal remains the same—to communicate your distinct attributes and prove that you are a good fit with the program. In the following tables, we present information on the types of admissions interviews conducted by top U.S. business schools. (Note: Data in these tables are based on information available on each school's Web site at the time of publication.)

Table A

School	Interview Process		Interview Type	
	Invitation	Applicant Initiated	Blind	Comprehensive
Chicago Booth	•		•	
Columbia Business School	•		•	
Cornell Johnson	•		•	
Dartmouth Tuck	•	•	•	
Duke Fuqua	•	•	•	
Harvard Business School	•			•
Michigan Ross	•		•	
MIT Sloan	•			•
Northwestern Kellogg	•	•	•	
NYU Stern	•			•
Stanford GSB	•		•	
UCLA Anderson	•		•	
UC-Berkeley Haas	•		•	
UPenn Wharton	•		•	
UVA Darden	•		•	
Yale	•		•	

Table B

School	Interviewer			Location	
	Admissions	Alumni	Student	On Campus	Off Campus
Chicago Booth	•	•	•	•	•
Columbia Business School		•			•
Cornell Johnson	•	•	•	•	•
Dartmouth Tuck	•	•	•	•	•
Duke Fuqua	•	•	•	•	•

Harvard Business School	•			•	•
Michigan Ross	•	•	•	•	•
MIT Sloan	•			•	•
Northwestern Kellogg	•	•	•	•	•
NYU Stern	•			•	•
Stanford GSB		•			•
UCLA Anderson			•		•
UC-Berkeley Haas		•	•	•	•
UPenn Wharton	•*		•*	•	•
UVA Darden	•		•	•	
Yale	•	•	•	•	•

Wharton's interviews now consist of an unmoderated team-based discussion with other candidates, plus a short one-on-one with an admissions officer or student.

WHAT WILL MY INTERVIEWER ASK?

MBA interviews are generally simple and straightforward. Candidates often fear that their interviewer will aggressively pepper them with challenging questions, but almost all interviews are friendly "get to know you" sessions, wherein you will be asked questions about your personal and professional history, career goals and reasons for applying to the particular school that is interviewing you. Which questions you ultimately receive and how they are presented will depend to some degree on whether your interview is "blind" or "comprehensive," and later in this guide, we present three complete sample interviews of each kind to illustrate the difference between them.

You will surely know the answers to the questions you are asked during your interview, because they will virtually always be about you and your experiences. You will never be asked, for example, to explain the theory of relativity or discuss economic policy in Namibia (unless, perhaps, you are a physicist or a specialist in Namibian economic policy!). Admissions interviews are not tests of your general knowledge or familiarity with a certain subject, but explorations of who you are as an individual and a professional. Your best strategy is to respond in a relaxed manner with the most natural, truthful and direct answer possible to the question asked.

Types of Questions

Open-Ended Questions

Open-ended questions—such as "Tell me about yourself," "Walk me through your résumé" and "Discuss your career progress since graduating from college"—are primarily used in blind interviews, because the interviewer has only minimal information with which to form meaningful questions. These types of questions essentially invite you to share whatever you feel is most important for the interviewer to know within a general topic area. Although receiving an open-ended question at a school that conducts comprehensive interviews is not impossible, we find that this happens very infrequently.

If you receive an open-ended query, it will typically be at the beginning of your interview. Although this initial question often serves as a foundation for the rest of the interview, at this point, your interviewer only wants to hear about the highlights of your life and career, with some insight into how you have made decisions and progressed. You therefore should not discuss every single project you have undertaken in every position you have ever held. If your interviewer is particularly interested in something you mention, he or she will ask follow-up questions and probe more deeply.

Career-Goals and Degree Questions

Some interview questions are designed to prod you for more information about your professional past and motivations for earning an advanced degree, like "What are your short- and long-term goals after graduating with your MBA?" and "Why do you need an MBA?" Generally, you should answer such questions in two to three minutes each and strive to balance conciseness with thoroughness.

As we discussed in Chapter 5, you cannot respond to questions about your post-MBA ambitions with a broad, seemingly unfounded statement like "I intend to go into consulting and then pursue academia." You will need to provide an appropriate level of detail that clarifies why the career choice suits you and why pursuing your stated goals after graduating with your MBA makes perfect sense, yet still keep your response rather short and simple. In general, concentrate on presenting yourself as a highly driven, focused and goal-oriented person who has done the proper research, but avoid getting caught up in minutiae. Consider the following response, which is still brief, yet notably more detailed:

> *As an equity research analyst, I have become a data junkie of sorts. I am constantly looking through numbers to find patterns and am enamored with "big data" and its application in marketing. After completing my MBA, I would like to join a marketing consulting firm, and ideally maintain my focus on retail marketing, with an industry leader like Envirosell. In the long term, after completing a variety of consulting assignments and establishing my credibility in the field, I expect to have been able to home in on a narrow area of interest within consumer marketing, and I ultimately aspire to teach analytical marketing at a business school while maintaining my own consulting practice.*

This candidate reveals that he is serious, directed and has a personality and background in line with his targeted career path. Of course, your goals will likely be different from these, but the kind of goal you choose for yourself is not what is most important—the details are!

School-Specific Questions

A very common business school interview question is "Why do you need an MBA *from our school?*" Understandably, schools want to know that you are not choosing their program because of superficial reasons, like rankings position or a legacy connection, but have truly researched how it best fits your personality and goals. An answer like "Columbia has a great entrepreneurship program and a significant student body so I can build my network," for example, would not be sufficient. It is simply too overarching and impersonal.

A persuasive response would cite specific features of the school and display your thorough knowledge of the program's particular benefits and culture:

> *When I first visited Columbia, I was immediately impressed by the school's commitment to entrepreneurship. To me, the opportunity to vet my ideas through the Entrepreneurial Sounding Board, gaining the critique of industry experts, is unprecedented. I would take that critical feedback, bolster my ideas and then apply to the Lang Center's Entrepreneurship Lab, which would give me both the cover and the community I would need to shepherd my idea along. Of course, beyond entrepreneurship, I love that Columbia is focused on building bonds between classmates even before school begins through the pre orientation trips and throughout the academic year with social trips and the Spring and Fall Balls. I want to be truly immersed in my MBA experience, academically and socially, and Columbia offers me vast opportunities to bond with like-minded students.*

Offering a detailed response in two minutes is entirely possible, and the best way to prepare yourself to do so is to refresh yourself before your interview on the school's strengths in your area of academic interest and need and on the school's culture and reputation.

Leadership, Professional Experience and Significant Accomplishments Questions

At most MBA programs, you will encounter questions about your career to date—and sometimes your extracurricular activities as well—with a particular focus on your leadership experience and/or your most compelling achievement(s) and significant moments. Such questions could include "What are your strengths and weaknesses as a leader?," "Of what accomplishment are you most proud?" and "Discuss a time when you led a team. How were you effective as a leader? What could you have done better?" Business schools are looking for candidates with communication skills, the ability to motivate others, compassion, the capacity to identify and solve complex interpersonal problems, a sense of humor and other such traits. These kinds of questions provide opportunities for candidates to reveal these qualities. Again, you should answer these questions in detail but also concisely—and most importantly, always offer real-life examples of your experiences to support any claims you make.

Responding, for example, with "As a leader I build communities and I am a clear communicator and goal-oriented implementer" would not be effective, because no evidence is provided (in the form of a related personal story) to validate these claims. By providing examples of times when you demonstrated the characteristics and skills you declare, you will establish legitimacy for your claims. Consider the following, more detailed response:

As a leader, I am effective at building communities. For example, during the economic crisis, our sales dropped substantially and morale *in our office likewise began to plummet. We found ourselves dealing with increasingly panicked and difficult clients. I could see the stress wearing on my teammates and prevailed upon our manager to allot $50 per week for—as silly as this might sound—what became known as "Bagel Friday at 10 a.m." Every Friday, everyone on the team would come in an hour late and have breakfast together. This gave us an extra hour of sleep and, more importantly, helped solidify the sense that we were all in it together as we swapped stories and laughed at our troubles. Even now, although our business has recovered, we maintain the tradition, because people look forward to connecting each week, and our team has never been stronger.*

"Fleshing out" your claims with relevant examples from your life makes your answers much more effective and persuasive—not to mention much more interesting.

This phase of questions will generally be very open and malleable. Candidates sometimes get flustered because they cannot, for example, come up with their "greatest accomplishment" on the spot. Whether your greatest accomplishment is when you took an entrepreneurial risk or when you raised $10K for charity does not matter—there is no "right" answer. Rather, the key is to respond intelligently, thoughtfully and thoroughly to the question asked.

Personal Questions

Because business schools are trying to gauge candidates' "fit" with their community as well as their academic and professional strengths, the admissions interview will often include a personal question or two, like "What do you do for fun?" or "What are your favorite hobbies and activities?" Again, these questions have no wrong answers.

Think to yourself how you would answer these questions if one of your friends were to ask them. Although discussing your private life in your interview may seem unusual, given that you are focused on your career goals and on getting into a particular MBA program, personal questions allow your interviewer to become more familiar with who you are as an individual, outside the work environment. Learning more about your interests and personality helps the interviewer better understand how—or even whether—you could contribute to the social atmosphere on campus. Simply relax, think and answer—and, where appropriate, tie your answer to certain extracurricular activities you could pursue at the school. For instance, the following would be a strong answer to the question "How do you most enjoy spending your free time?":

> *I love playing ice hockey—I first skated on the frozen pond at my grandparents' farm when I was just four years old, and I have skated regularly ever since. I joined my first hockey team when I was seven, and I still play twice a week with a group of friends. I am really excited that XYZ School has a student hockey team, because I would love to maintain this hobby while I am studying—it's also a great stress reliever—and it would be a wonderful way to meet friends and bond with some of my classmates.*

Notice how this answer is concise yet detailed, how it includes real-life examples from the applicant's past and present, and links directly with the school's extracurricular offerings. Constantly relating your experiences to your target school's resources can become tiresome, however, so be careful not to overdo it and to keep such references relevant and believable.

Your Questions

Most interviewers will leave time for you to ask a few questions in return. Note that this is *not* the time to learn basic information about the school (you should know the school "inside and out" before you arrive), however, but an opportunity to ask insightful questions that inferentially showcase your knowledge of the school or confirm that you are critically evaluating your options. For example, asking, "What entrepreneurial programs do you have?" would not reflect well on you. If you are interested in entrepreneurship, you should already be well versed in the school's resources in this area. However, you could ask, for example, "The new dean has been in place for six months now. Would you say that the school has changed in any significant way during this time?" Such a question shows that you are staying informed about what is happening on campus and are genuinely eager to learn more—you have really been doing your research and considering your options. A quick rule of thumb is that if the answer to your question can be easily found on the program's Web site or in its promotional materials, your question is not nuanced enough to be appropriate for this opportunity.

Avoid overarching exploratory questions ("What should I know about your finance program?") and vague questions with no direct connection to your goals ("What do *you* like about the business school?"), while also keeping in mind who your interviewer is. Alumni may not know specifics about recent changes to curriculum or budgets on campus, for example, whereas admissions personnel may not have as much insight into how the MBA comes into play in the workplace (as an alumnus/ alumna would).

Be sure to have multiple questions in mind to show that you have done more than the minimum to prepare and also so you have backup queries, in case your first-choice questions are naturally answered during the course of your interview. Take the time and do the "digging" necessary to ensure that your questions pertain to information you need and genuinely want to know. The school's press releases can bring you up to speed on important announcements and initiatives and can thus be great sources of inspiration when you are brainstorming possible question topics. (mbaMission's Insider Guides can also be useful in providing inspiration.) Remember, though, that the questions you formulate using information from these sources should ideally relate to you, your candidacy and your stated educational and career goals.

SAMPLE BLIND INTERVIEWS

We have now discussed the most common types of questions you can expect to receive in your admissions interview, but how might these questions be presented in a typical "blind" interview? To answer that question, we present here two complete sample interviews from past applicants to schools that use the "blind" approach.

Sample Blind Interview 1:

- How did you get to this point in your career? Do you have any particular experiences you would like to share?

- Walk me through your résumé.

- Why do you feel you need an MBA now?

- Why is our school the right one for you?

- List your top three strengths.

- List your top three weaknesses.

- What is unique about you?

- How will you contribute to our school?

- Do you have any questions for me or about our school?

Sample Blind Interview 2:

- Walk me through your résumé.

- Why the transition from X to Y firm? What was different from your prior company experience? *(Follow-up question based on applicant's response to the first question.)*

- Tell me about the role you typically play on a team.

- Tell me about a leadership experience. What traits does this experience reveal about you?

- What do you not like about your current group at work?

- Why do you need an MBA?

- Why did you choose our school?

- What activities or clubs will you partake in?

- How do you plan to contribute in class?

- Do you have any questions for me?

Sample Blind Interview 3:

- What led you to where you are today?

- Why do you need an MBA and why now?

- Why have you chosen our career programs?

- What are your career goals?

- If your career goals were not to work out, what is your Plan B?

- Why is teamwork important to you?

- Tell me about a time when you failed/made a mistake.

- What clubs/leadership opportunities are you interested in at our school?

- What concentrations would you pursue?

- What do you do in your free time/for fun?

- Is there anything we did not cover that you wish to tell me? Anything you wish I had asked you?

- Do you have any questions for me?

SAMPLE COMPREHENSIVE INTERVIEWS

Many applicants are fearful of comprehensive interviews, because they expect (wrongly!) the interviewer to nitpick his or her way through their application, asking narrow (or even accusatory) questions about grades, GMAT scores and the like. Rest assured, this is not the case. A comprehensive interviewer is not a detective seeking to poke holes in your case and uncover a reason to reject you, but a regular person just trying to obtain a more complete picture of you and your candidacy. Because comprehensive interviews are tailored to each applicant, offering generalizations about them is difficult. To help illustrate how these interviews can go, we present here three complete sample interviews from past candidates at schools that use the "comprehensive" approach:

Sample Comprehensive Interview 1:

- How did you become head of marketing?

- What was your marketing strategy?

- How did you know how to get a product produced?

- How many people were on your team?

- How did you walk away from a company you helped build? Tell me about your thought process.

- Tell me about your current job. Was the transition to this new role a tough one?

- How did you handle it?

- What do you do now day to day?

- Tell me more.

- Tell me about a typical day in your life outside of work.

Sample Comprehensive Interview 2:

- Tell me about your college small business and what you learned from it.

- What about your current position keeps you up at night—if anything?

- Explain a work concept to me in simple terms, as if I were a layman.

- What are your strengths and weaknesses?

- Tell me more about your career plan—what you would like to be doing three to five years out and what you would like to do in the long run.

- What is missing between who you are now and the CEO you want to be? How are you developing these traits?

- What do you think you will struggle with while in business school?

- Walk me through a typical day at work.

- How do you keep current with the news?

- Is there anything you were hoping to talk about but have not had a chance to?

Sample Comprehensive Interview 3:

- Assume I had not read your application or résumé—tell me about yourself.

- You are very independent; is that an asset or a liability in investment banking?

- How do you work in a team? What if a team member disagrees with you?

- Tell me about a situation when you led a team.

- You talked a lot about community; how do you "break into" a community?

- Your recommenders mentioned that you connect particularly well with CEOs and CFOs of companies you talk to. Why do you think that is?

- Who is the most interesting person you have worked with? Describe him or her.

- What does a typical day look like for you?

- How have you changed since college?

- Have you visited campus?

- What do you think makes our school different?

GROUP INTERVIEWS

Another kind of interview you may face on your admissions journey is the group interview, though at this point, such interviews are still very rare. In fact, the Wharton School at the University of Pennsylvania is the only top MBA program to have initiated such sessions. Although Wharton has reported on its blog that the new process—in which admissions officers observe a discussion/debate among a group of six applicants at a time—has been productive and helpful in its decision making, whether this process will be adopted by other schools is still unclear.

For now, Wharton has made its group interview prompts publicly available, though these could of course change at any point:

- What is one key business skill that you think post-business school professionals must have in order to be successful, long-term, in their career?

- What is the most important societal challenge that could be addressed more effectively by the business community today?

The key to successfully managing the group interview—which at Wharton is unmoderated at this point, meaning that the applicants are asked a question and given time to discuss it without any imperative to reach a consensus or achieve an objective—is to act with thoughtfulness and diplomacy.

Approach a group discussion/interview just as you would a business school class. Being the first or the dominant speaker is not imperative. Instead, focus on listening and making a few strong, clearly conveyed points—think quality rather than quantity. In addition, being supportive of others, ensuring that they are heard or their points clarified, should score you some points. Of course, this will require judgment, but if you enter the discussion with the proper mind-set, you should be able to effectively showcase your temperament and character.

. . . .

ADMISSIONS MYTHS DESTROYED: I MUST INTERVIEW WITH THE ADMISSIONS COMMITTEE!

After submitting your application, you endure weeks of nervous anticipation and then finally get that invitation to interview. You prepare for the interview and you book your flight to campus, ready to prove yourself to the admissions committee. You take a campus tour, sit in on a class and head to the admissions office only to find... (*gasp!*) a second-year student waiting to interview you—and he is wearing jeans! Before you assume that the school could not possibly be taking you seriously or has classified you in some second tier of candidates that it does not really care about, take a deep breath and reconsider.

The admissions committee's job is to find the best candidates for the school's MBA program. So, whether you interview with someone from the admissions office, an alumnus/alumna or a student, your interview is just as important as that of every other applicant who interviews with the school and will be treated exactly the same by the admissions committee. Why would an admissions committee bother organizing interviews with applicants it does not intend to earnestly consider? What would be the point of engaging the school's alumni to meet with candidates if the admissions committee did not feel the school's graduates were reliable judges of potential students? Why would an admissions committee solicit interview help from the school's students if these students were not capable of appropriately evaluating applicants?

If you find yourself on campus and interviewing with someone other than an admissions committee member, do not be disheartened or lose your focus. Your candidacy will be fairly and impartially weighed, no matter who is sitting across from you. Remember, your story and your ability to connect with your interviewer are far more important than anything else.

• •

How Do I Prepare?

Know Your Story

As we noted earlier, your interview will be primarily—if not exclusively—about you. The best way to be ready to respond to any possible question, then, is to prepare to discuss the parts of your academic, professional and personal life that you feel are most significant and indicative of both the person you are today and the person you are striving to become in the future. The most important rule in preparing for *any* MBA interview is therefore this: *Know your story.*

If you have been invited to interview, several weeks or even months may have passed since you submitted your application. We strongly recommend, then, that before meeting with your interviewer, you reacquaint yourself with your story as you presented it to the school: review your résumé, essays and application form so that you are ready to discuss the specific ambitions, experiences, achievements and other details and themes featured in these documents. If you are interviewing at a school *before* submitting your application, you must determine your key stories in advance of your meeting. Start by deciding what overall image of yourself you want to convey. Then, identify events and aspects within your history that best support this image by going through your résumé and reminding yourself of the details behind each position and accomplishment. You should be able to discuss with ease the three or four top reasons (1) you want/need an MBA at this point of your life and (2) you want to go to the school at which you are interviewing.

Time Management

During your interview, time management is critical. Interviews are typically 30 minutes long, and most interviewers will have a list of questions prepared (sometimes a hard-copy list and at other times just a mental agenda) and want to get through the entire list in the time allotted. If you ramble on and take ten minutes to answer one question, you will give the impression that you lack self-awareness and may talk too much in class or in team situations. Perhaps even more importantly, limiting the interviewer's capacity to ask additional questions by using too much time to respond can prevent you from being able to offer other critical or interesting information about yourself.

Whether you choose to employ mbaMission for a mock interview or practice on your own in a mirror, we strongly recommend that you actually vocalize your responses and not just write them out on paper. Further, we suggest that you use a timer to get a sense of how long it takes you to answer each practice question—you would be surprised at how quickly two or three minutes can go by.

Conversation, Not Memorization

Do not memorize or overplan your responses. Your goal is to be conversational, not robotic. Questions can come in many forms, and candidates who memorize potential answers tend to have trouble adjusting to questions that are asked in a new, different or otherwise unexpected way. In our experience, this is particularly relevant for open-ended questions.

Viewing a Story from Different Angles

After you have identified your most significant stories and points, you will need to be ready to capitalize on good opportunities to share this information during your interview. Obviously, you will not know in advance exactly which questions your interviewer will ask, so you cannot assign specific stories to specific questions. Instead, you will need to consider beforehand the different contexts within which you can discuss each item, so that when a related question arises, you already know which anecdote or point would make a compelling response. If, for example, your experience as a youth soccer coach is an important story for you, you could work it into the interview as an example of leadership, teamwork, personal interests, conflict resolution, community contribution or even a setback or failure when a question on one of these topics is asked. Your stories are far more flexible than you might realize and can be "spun" in various ways as needed.

Think of five to six key points (activities, personality traits, etc.) you absolutely want to be sure you get across during your interview. Then think about possible questions to which you can "hook" those points. For example, if you spend one afternoon a week tutoring inmates for their GED, potential "hook" questions could be as follows:

• Tell me about a time when you demonstrated initiative.

> Example: *"I wanted to make a difference but wanted to move beyond just helping high school students. So I researched where in my area the biggest need was and found a program that brings volunteers to prisons to . . . ."*

• Tell me about a time when you went above and beyond.

Example: *"For the past few years, I have been engaged in some meaningful service—teaching GED prep in a local prison. I was surprised to find that inmates were only allowed to attend one hour of extra tutoring per week. Recognizing that my students needed additional help, I devoted extensive time and effort to develop a series of math and vocabulary flash cards for them to use in between sessions. My additional efforts showed them that I truly was committed to their success. Further, the students found them to be extremely helpful—all five of them passed the GED that year!"*

- Tell me about a time when you had to motivate a reluctant person.

  Example: *"My best example I believe occurred outside the office, as part of my volunteer work with inmates studying for their GED. Although most of the inmates I tutor are very motivated, once in a while I work with someone who … ."*

- What do you think you could bring to campus?

  Example: *"With the inmates I tutor on a volunteer basis, I have to break down complex concepts into simple terms, and I believe I've become quite good at doing this. I believe at XYZ School, I could help my fellow classmates struggling in certain classes by taking this same approach."*

We must clarify, however, that we are *not* suggesting that you answer four different questions with the same story; we are merely illustrating how a single element of your profile can be used for multiple questions. By selecting several key personal stories and examining them from different angles before your meeting, you can better ensure that you will find a way to share them during the interview.

FREQUENTLY ASKED QUESTIONS

1. Does a school-initiated interview (i.e., invitation) carry more weight than an applicant-initiated interview?

No, schools consider both options equal. However, when a school offers the option of scheduling an interview, we recommend that you reserve a spot on its interview calendar as soon as possible. In particularly competitive years, interview slots can fill up quickly, and you do not want to miss out on a chance to interview!

2. Does it matter if I travel to campus to interview or meet with a local alumnus/alumna to do so?

An on-campus interview (with a member of the admissions office or a student) and an interview with a graduate of the school in your area carry the same weight. However, we recommend that applicants who have not yet visited their target school and do not live overseas use the interview as an opportunity—if at all possible—to travel to campus, attend a class and perhaps meet and/or have lunch with a student. You will be able to speak far more intelligently about your target program after a visit.

3. What should I wear?

Always follow any guidelines the school provides on proper interview dress. If "business casual" is specified, wear business casual; if "business attire," dress in business attire. Jeans, T-shirts and ripped or unclean clothing are never appropriate. If the school does not specify a dress code, wear business attire for any on-campus interviews as well as for an off-campus interview with a member of the admissions staff. Business casual is often best when meeting an alumnus/alumna off campus, though you may consider politely asking the person you are meeting about proper attire in advance. Showing some creativity and style with your clothing is okay, but do not go overboard— remember that your meeting is essentially a professional one, and you want to make a good impression.

> *A Note About Skype Interviews*: If you do a Skype interview, you should treat it just as you would an in-person interview, including dressing the part. Find a quiet place where you will not be interrupted and where your Internet connection is clear and dependable. Clear away any clutter from the area where you will be seated and turn off or remove all possible sources of distraction (e.g., television, radio, pets) so you can give your interviewer your undivided attention. In all ways, conduct yourself in a professional manner, as though you were truly face-to-face with your interviewer.

4. I am meeting my interviewer at a coffee shop. Who pays?

If you are meeting an alumnus/alumna at a café or similar establishment for an interview, you can avoid the awkward "who pays?" scenario by arriving early, purchasing your own beverage and then offering to pay for the interviewer's selection when he or she arrives. If your interviewer arrives before you, you might politely offer to pay for his or her drink, but if your offer is declined, you should not insist.

5. Should I send a thank you note?

Always write a thank you letter to your interviewer—they can establish continuity and are an easy way of reinforcing a positive impression or relationship. These days, emailing your note is entirely acceptable and even advisable. Interviewers usually must submit their feedback on candidates within 24–48 hours, so you want your message to be received quite quickly. If you wait—or choose to send your note via conventional mail, which is simply too slow—your interviewer's report may have already been submitted, and you will have missed this valuable opportunity to make an additional positive impression.

TIPS FOR WHEN YOU FIND YOURSELF TONGUE-TIED

Many business school applicants worry that their interviewer will ask a challenging question that leaves them awkwardly silent—and that this would essentially end their candidacy at the school. Although this scenario would certainly be uncomfortable, we can assure you that an awkward pause in an interview will not cancel out all the positive elements of your profile. Still, being ready for such a situation is key, so we offer the following tips on how to navigate an awkward moment:

- *Resist the urge to launch into a story*: Your instinct may be to just start speaking, hoping that you will find the right story as you progress. This is a high-risk strategy, however, because it can actually compound the problem by depriving you of a chance to think clearly and identify the best option for the situation. Instead, allow yourself a pensive pause and perhaps even say, "That is a good question. I am going to have to think about it for a moment," to buy yourself a few extra seconds of reflection before committing to an answer.

- *Take a sip of water*: If your interviewer offers you a glass of water at the beginning of your meeting, take it and use it as needed throughout the interview to buy time or slow yourself down. Taking a sip of water offers you a brief moment to pause naturally and think about your answer a little more before responding.

- *Take a pass*: If you absolutely cannot answer a question, do not become overly apologetic or start making excuses. Simply acknowledge that you are having trouble with the question and politely ask if you might come back to it at the end. This is not a best-case scenario, but it is far better than rambling and apologizing.

- *Maintain your poise*: If you struggle with a question, let the moment go as quickly as possible and redirect your focus onto the next query. Continuing to dwell on it will only distract you and complicate your efforts to respond to any subsequent questions. If instead you confidently move on and make the best of the rest of the interview, you should be able to overcome a single awkward moment.

Rest assured that your interviewer is not out to fool or trick you. As we have noted, most of the questions you will receive will probe your life and experiences. Getting a question that is designed to trip you up is exceedingly rare.

Typical MBA Candidate Interview Questions

General Introductory Questions:

1. Tell me about yourself.

2. Walk me through your résumé. Briefly explain your roles/responsibilities in each of your positions and the specific dates of these positions.

3. Discuss your career progress since your graduation from college.

4. Tell me about your parents and family. Where do you come from?

5. Tell me about your life.

6. Tell me about your career.

7. What are your short-term and long-term career goals?

8. In what positions do you see yourself right after graduation and five years later?

9. Walk me through your career goals.

10. Why do you want/need an MBA to achieve your goals?

11. Why our MBA program?

Career (for illustrative purposes, some of the questions in this section assume the candidate's career goals involve being a consultant, but they can easily be adapted for any other career goals):

12. What is general management?

13. What does a consultant do?

14. Why do you want to be a consultant?

15. What will you get out of your consulting experience? How will this help you reach the next stage of your career?

16. Can you be specific in defining your post-MBA career objectives?

17. Can you be specific in describing your goals as a consultant?

18. What skills do you have that will enable you to excel in this role?

19. What challenges do you anticipate in your career?

20. Aside from earning your MBA, how will you prepare for this career?

21. What skills will you gain from an MBA that will enable you to excel in this role?

22. Why do you need an MBA? Could you continue with your existing job and still achieve your goals?

23. How, specifically, can our program help you with your long-term goals?

24. What motivates you?

25. What will you do if you do not get into an MBA program this year?

Professional Experience:

26. What do you do exactly in your position?

27. Walk me through your responsibilities in your current position.

28. What do you like the most about your current job?

29. What do you like the least about your current job?

30. What do you find meaningful about your current position?

31. Describe a success and a failure you have experienced in your current position.

32. Tell me about a time you had to work with someone with whom you did not get along. Tell me more about the actual confrontation and how you handled it.

33. How do you manage your boss?

34. How have you taught those who are junior to you?

35. What accomplishment on your résumé are you most proud of?

36. What is the current status of your company? What will happen to or within the company if you pursue your MBA? (for entrepreneurs, in particular)

37. Did you have opportunities to work for other companies after college? If so, why did you choose to accept a position at your current company?

38. XYZ must be great company to work for. What do you like about it?

39. Tell me about something from your current job that occurred within the past few months that most intrigued you.

40. Tell me about a professional regret or mistake.

41. How will you continue learning in your next position?

Leadership/Teamwork:

42. What do you think are the qualities of a leader? Tell me about a time you displayed leadership.

43. What do you think are the most important elements of a high-performing team?

44. What do you think it is about your personality that gives you the ability to interact with diverse types of people, business partners, etc.?

45. Discuss an example of when you displayed leadership. How were you a successful leader?

46. What makes you good at your job? What are your strengths?

47. What makes a great leader, and what characteristics must a leader project to employees to be effective?

48. How do you think you can have an impact on a team/business without holding a leadership role? Give an example of a time when you made a difference in such a non-leadership role.

49. Recall a specific time when you encountered team conflicts (i.e., conflicts among individuals within a team). What did you do to resolve the conflict?

50. How do you function in a team?

51. How do you lead a group?

52. Pick two words that would describe what you would not do in a team setting.

53. If you did not agree with a team member, how would you approach the situation?

54. If you had a team member who was contributing less than other team members, what would you do to motivate him or her?

55. What is your definition of leadership? Relate it to a leadership experience.

56. What would your current teammates say about you, and would you agree with their assessment?

57. What kind of relationship do you have with your managers? Do you always agree?

58. Please provide an example from work when you were asked to come up with an innovative idea. What were the results?

59. What characteristics do you think a good leader should have?

60. Tell me about a leader you admire and why.

61. How would your subordinates describe you?

62. What skills would you bring to a learning team or study group?

63. Discuss an ethical challenge that you have faced at the office.

64. Tell me about a time when you disagreed with your manager. How did you manage your relationship? What were the implications?

65. How and when do you seek the advice of others?

66. How would you describe your risk tolerance?

Personal:

67. You have made many decisions, both large and small, in your life. If you could change one decision, what would it be and why?

68. Going from working to studying is a big change. How will you prepare yourself, or how have you already prepared yourself?

69. How would your friends describe you?

70. In what extracurricular activities were you involved during college?

71. What was your most difficult personal hurdle, and how did you overcome it?

72. What are three principles that you hold dear and why?

73. Why did you choose your undergraduate program?

74. Would you do anything differently in your undergraduate studies if given the opportunity?

75. What is unique about you?

76. What else would you like to tell me about you?

77. What will you do if you are not accepted into our school?

78. What is the last book you read?

79. What global issue is most important to you?

80. Where have you traveled?

81. How do you connect with others when you travel?

Specific to the School:

82. What specifically about our program attracted you to it?

83. How did you learn about our program?

84. Have you visited our classrooms? If so, what did you think?

85. Have you spoken to any of our current students or to any alumni?

86. If you were accepted, which extracurricular activities would you participate in?

87. If you were accepted, which country would you choose to study in/visit and why?

88. What concerns do you have about attending our school?

89. Why us? Please do not tell me the typical reasons that every candidate cites.

90. What unique contribution will you make in our classroom?

91. What unique contributions will you make in our social/cultural environment?

92. To which other schools have you applied?

93. What aspect of your application worries you the most?

94. What do you believe is the greatest strength of your candidacy? Weakness?

95. If you came back to this school in 15 years for a class reunion, what would your classmates remember about you?

96. What will be the key difference between your life now and your life when you are a student at our school?

Final Questions from the Interviewer:

97. If you had one minute to directly address the admissions committee, what would you say?

98. Would you like to discuss anything specific in your application?

99. Do you have any questions for me?

100. What else would you like the admissions committee to know about you?

APPENDIX A

A SPECIAL EXERCISE FOR CAREER CHANGERS

A SPECIAL EXERCISE FOR CAREER CHANGERS

As we noted earlier, many business school applicants are interested in earning their MBA as a way of changing careers. Although schools recognize this trend, they also have to satisfy the needs of their recruiters, most of whom come to campus to hire applicants who already have depth of experience in their field—even more so during difficult economic times, when they tend to become increasingly conservative in their hiring practices. Even when hiring is robust, however, career changers in particular need to be able to prove that they "fit" with their new target career. To effectively do so, they must highlight the components of their past that have provided them with applicable foundational experience or transferable skills for their future career. We have created a worksheet that will help you

- determine the skills and past experiences you should emphasize in your personal statement that will demonstrate continuity, themes and transferable skills.

- think through your short-term goals.

- distill your personal statement down to a one-page snapshot, which you will use as a guide.

Both a completed sample worksheet and a blank one appear on the following pages. To complete the worksheet, follow these eight steps:

1. Enter a summary statement of your long-term goal in Box A, labeled "Long-Term Goal." The reason for starting at the end in this way is to help keep you focused on your ultimate vision of where you want to be with your career; this will in turn help you decide which skills or traits you will need to be able to attain that goal (and which you will need to emphasize in your essay).

269

2. In Box B, the "Skills/Traits" box directly underneath the "Long-Term Goal" box, list eight to ten skills or traits you will need to be successful in pursuing your long-term goal. These can include skills/traits you already have as well as ones you do not yet possess. Think about "hard" skills, like financial analysis or expertise in writing business plans, as well as "soft" skills, like the ability to motivate or inspire others.

The purpose of this box is for you to think creatively and comprehensively about what competencies you need to achieve your goal. By then looking at which competencies you already have and which ones you still need (as you will do in completing the following steps), you will clarify what you will need to emphasize in your personal statement.

3. In Box C, the "Skills/Traits" box directly underneath Box D, "Experience," list which of the skills/traits you identified in Step 2 you already possess (i.e., that you have gained from your professional, community or personal experiences). Note: this list should be shorter than the list in Step 2, because in this case, you are listing only those skills/traits that you can already claim. The goal of this step is to determine which of your current competencies are important for your long-term goal; these are the traits you will emphasize in your personal statement. For example, let us say that one such trait is an ability to motivate a team, and you do not have any work-related team leadership experience. However, you were captain of a championship basketball team in college. You might not originally have thought of mentioning that college experience, but by listing in Step 2 all the traits you need for your long-term goal, you now know that this team leadership experience is in fact relevant.

4. In Box D, labeled "Experience," enter a summary statement of the specific experiences that relate to the skills/traits you just listed in Step 3. Using our example from Step 3, in this box, you would list your experience as captain of the championship-winning college basketball team.

5. In Box E, the "Skills/Traits" box located directly underneath Box F, "MBA," list which skills/traits you expect to gain from earning your MBA degree. Note that this list will be shorter than the list in Step 2, because in this case, you are detailing only those skills/traits you still need to gain. The purpose of this list is to help you identify aspects of the school—specific classes, clubs, excursions, other resources—that will help prepare you to pursue your goals.

6. In Box F, the "MBA" box, summarize the list you just created in Step 5 into a description of what you want to gain from your MBA experience.

7. Look now at the list of skills/traits that you listed in Box B (Step 2) and cross off any that you have listed in Step 3 (those you already possess) or Step 5 (those you will gain in business school). Which skills/traits are left? Those missing skills/traits are what you need your short-term goal to provide. List these in Box G, labeled "Skills/Traits," directly underneath Box H, "Short-Term Goal."

8. In Box H, labeled "Short-Term Goal," write a summary statement of your short-term goal. Ideally, your short-term goal will provide you with the skills/traits listed in Box G (Step 7).

When you have completed these steps, what you will have is a one-page snapshot of your personal statement. This worksheet will help you avoid simply repeating elements from your résumé or using up your allotted word count relating experiences that are not connected to your goals. It will help you tell a story that has continuity and that clearly emphasizes which skills you already have and which you still need to obtain. Although you most likely will not—and probably should not—write the essay linearly (as the information now appears on your worksheet), being able to see all the key components of the essay in one place is extremely helpful and helps ensure that you have addressed all the necessary points.

Sample Completed Worksheet

This worksheet will help you accomplish the following:

1. Determine the skills and past experiences you should emphasize in your personal statement that will demonstrate continuity, themes and transferable skills.
2. Think through your short-term goals.
3. Distill your personal statement down to a one-page snapshot, which you will use as a guide.

D. Experience	F. MBA	H. Short-Term Goal	A. Long-Term Goal
Operations major, worked for three years in China, spent childhood in developing country	Must focus on finance, HR, consulting and build skills in these areas; join clubs for hands-on experience	Obtain position consulting in a developing country	To consult with factories in developing countries on operational improvements

C. Skills/Traits:	E. Skills/Traits:	G. Skills/Traits:	B. Skills/Traits:
• English, Chinese • Operations experience in China • Empathy/ no judgment (childhood perspective) • Leading team at work; developed motivation skills	• Volunteer, Consulting Club = first hand knowledge • Finance skills – Finance Club • Alumni network • Take electives on HR challenges in other countries	• Work for Bain/BCG in China, Ops division •Find mentor I can learn motivation skills from •Improve operational knowledge	• Consulting and teaching skills • Languages (English, Chinese, Indonesian) • Finance skills • Motivational techniques • Ability to suspend judgment, empathy • HR tools & knowledge • Operations experience

Blank Worksheet

This worksheet will help you accomplish the following:
1. Determine the skills and past experiences you should emphasize in your personal statement that will demonstrate continuity, themes and transferable skills.
2. Think through your short-term goals.
3. Distill your personal statement down to a one-page snapshot, which you will use as a guide.

D. Experience	F. MBA	H. Short-Term Goal	A. Long-Term Goal

C. Skills/Traits:	E. Skills/Traits:	G. Skills/Traits:	B. Skills/Traits:

Box A: Enter a summary statement of your long-term goal.

Box B: List eight to ten skills/traits you will need to be successful in attaining your long-term goal.

Box C: List which of the skills/traits in Box B you have already gained from your professional, community or personal experiences.

Box D: Enter a summary statement of the specific experiences that relate to the skills/traits in Box C.

Box E: List the skills/traits you expect to gain from earning your MBA degree.

Box F: Summarize the list from Box E into a description of what you want from your MBA experience.

Box G: List the skills from Box B that have not been listed in Boxes C or E.

Box H: Enter a summary statement of your short-term goal.

APPENDIX B

ACTION-ORIENTED VERBS

List of Action-Oriented Verbs That Help Show Accomplishments, Rather Than Responsibilities

A

Accelerated

Accomplished

Achieved

Activated

Adapted

Addressed

Adjusted

Advanced

Advocated

Allocated

Answered

Applied

Appraised

Approved

Arbitrated

Arranged

Ascertained

Assembled

Assessed

Assigned

Attained

Augmented

Authorized

Awarded

B

Balanced

Boosted

Briefed

Budgeted

Built

C

Calculated

Captured

Cataloged

Centralized

Chaired

Charted

Clarified

Classified

Coached

Collaborated

Collected

Combined

Communicated

Compared

Compiled

Completed

Composed

Conceived

Conceptualized

Condensed

Conducted

Conferred

Conserved

Consolidated

Constructed

Contacted

Continued

Controlled

Converted

Convinced

Coordinated

Corresponded

Counseled

Created

Critiqued

Cultivated

Customized

D

Decided

Defined

Delegated

Delivered

Demonstrated

Designated

Designed

Detected

Determined

Developed

Devised

Diagnosed

Directed

Discovered

Displayed

Distributed

Diverted

Documented

Drafted

E

Earned

Edited

Educated	**F**	Honed	Issued
Eliminated	Fabricated	Hosted	**J**
Emphasized	Facilitated	**I**	Joined
Employed	Fashioned	Identified	Judged
Encouraged	Finalized	Illustrated	**L**
Enforced	Fixed	Imagined	Launched
Engineered	Focused	Implemented	Learned
Enhanced	Forecasted	Improved	Lectured
Enlarged	Formed	Improvised	Led
Enlisted	Formulated	Incorporated	Lifted
Ensured	Fostered	Increased	Listened
Entertained	Found	Influenced	Located
Established	Fulfilled	Informed	Logged
Estimated	Furnished	Initiated	**M**
Evaluated	**G**	Innovated	Maintained
Examined	Gained	Inspected	Managed
Executed	Gathered	Installed	Marketed
Expanded	Generated	Instituted	Maximized
Expedited	Governed	Integrated	Measured
Experimented	Grossed	Interacted	Mediated
Explained	Guided	Interpreted	Merged
Explored	**H**	Interviewed	Mobilized
Expressed	Handled	Introduced	Modified
Extended	Headed	Invented	Monitored
Extracted	Heightened	Investigated	Motivated
	Hired	Involved	

N

Navigated

Negotiated

Netted

O

Obtained

Opened

Operated

Ordered

Orchestrated

Organized

Originated

Outlined

Overcame

Overhauled

Oversaw

P

Performed

Persuaded

Piloted

Pinpointed

Pioneered

Placed

Planned

Played

Predicted

Prepared

Prescribed

Presented

Presided

Prevented

Prioritized

Processed

Produced

Programmed

Projected

Promoted

Proposed

Protected

Proved

Provided

Publicized

Purchased

Q

Qualified

Questioned

R

Raised

Ran

Reached

Realized

Reasoned

Received

Recommended

Reconciled

Recorded

Recruited

Reduced

Referred

Regulated

Rehabilitated

Related

Rendered

Reorganized

Repaired

Replaced

Reported

Represented

Researched

Reshaped

Resolved

Responded

Restored

Retrieved

Reviewed

Revised

Revitalized

Routed

S

Saved

Screened

Searched

Secured

Selected

Served

Shaped

Shared

Simplified

Simulated

Sketched

Sold

Solved

Sorted

Spearheaded

Specialized

Specified

Spoke

Sponsored

Staffed

Standardized

Started

Streamlined

Strengthened

Structured

Studied

Suggested

Summarized

Supervised

Supplied

Supported

Surpassed

Surveyed

Sustained

Synthesized

T

Targeted

Taught

Tested

Tracked

Traded

Trained

Transcribed

Transformed

Translated

Transmitted

Tutored

U

Uncovered

Undertook

Unified

United

Updated

Upgraded

Used

Utilized

V

Validated

Verbalized

Verified

Volunteered

W

Weighed

Won

Worked

Wrote

APPENDIX C

THE WAITLIST

THE WAITLIST

"You have been placed on our waitlist."

In some ways, those seven words are more dreaded by business school candidates than a straightforward rejection, because spending time on a school's waitlist means that the agony of waiting for a decision is somewhat indefinite. Admissions committees rarely indicate when they believe a final decision will be rendered, so you just might remain in admissions purgatory for months. Still, as frustrating as this situation can be, there *is* hope. Although being placed on a program's waitlist is certainly not as satisfying as being accepted, it does mean that the admissions committee likes what it sees and does not want to lose the opportunity to have you in the school's next class. Indeed, admissions committees have waitlists not to torment innocent applicants but so they can maintain the option of accepting certain candidates in the future as the incoming class takes shape. So, if you find yourself on your target school's waitlist, do your best to see the glass as half full, as they say.

Unfortunately, waitlist processes tend to be pretty opaque. Most top schools are loathe to release information regarding the number of applicants on their waitlist and the number of candidates they expect to ultimately accept from that list, for fear that waitlisted applicants will either lose interest or give up and make other plans. Further, virtually all schools state that they do not rank waitlist applicants; this seems logical, given that the school wants the right to continuously evaluate candidates against others in the incoming class and to make their admissions decisions as the class takes shape.

When you apply naturally affects when you are placed on the waitlist, and this in turn influences when you might receive a final decision from the school. If you are placed on the waitlist after Round 1, you will typically be reevaluated along with the Round 2 applicants. If you are waitlisted after Round 2 (or even waitlisted again!), you will typically be reevaluated along with candidates who submit in Round 3. If you find yourself on the waitlist after Round 3 decisions have been made, you will no longer be evaluated along with the general applicant pool but will be held in a kind of holding pattern as the school waits to see which of its offers are accepted. So, as the application season progresses, you will shift from hoping that you fit in with the class to hoping that someone else chooses not to accept his or her admissions offer so that a spot will open up for you.

Over the past few years, schools have become a little bit more transparent about how they manage their waitlists. Most programs provide FAQs about their waitlist process, and if your target school does so, this information will be included in the decision email it sends out. The admissions committee's FAQs will outline very deliberate instructions on what you should and should not do after being placed on the waitlist. This brings us to the most important rule of proper waitlist etiquette: *Listen to the admissions committee.*

THE CLOSED WAITLIST

If the school tells you not to send follow-up material of any sort, this means the program maintains a "closed" waitlist. In this case, you should absolutely *not* yield to temptation and send files or other items that you think will bolster your candidacy and give you an advantage over your peers. If you ignore the school's directive and (misguidedly) choose to provide additional information or documents anyway, you will only succeed in identifying yourself in a negative way. This is most definitely *not* the kind of message you want to send to a group that will be determining your fate.

Among the top schools that maintain a closed waitlist is the Stanford Graduate School of Business. A sample Stanford waitlist decision letter follows:

This letter may be the most frustrating of all to receive. It does not offer you admission to the Master of Business Administration Program at the Stanford Graduate School of Business, nor does it tell you that we cannot offer you admission. It is a "waitpool" letter.

Your application for admission to the Stanford MBA Program for Fall 2013 was impressive. Unfortunately, the number of candidates to whom we would like to offer admission exceeds the number of available places in the class. We ask for your patience as we determine whether we will be able to offer you admission to the MBA Class of 2015. If you decide to accept a place in the waitpool, we will review your file again, along with those of other candidates in the waitpool, and post an updated decision on 27 March 2013.

Candidates in the waitpool are not ranked. As such, we cannot predict your chances of being admitted. We can promise that your file will receive another thorough and careful review if you choose to remain in the waitpool. We hope that you will do so. Please accept a place in the waitpool by submitting the online Waitpool Candidate Reply Form by 6 February 2013. While we are unable to speak individually with you to discuss your candidacy, we hope that the following information will answer your questions and provide you with more details about the waitpool. Thank you for your patience and cooperation in adhering to the waitpool procedure.

I apologize for prolonging what already may seem a long and drawn-out process, but please know that you are still a competitive candidate for admission. Thank you for your patience, and for your interest in the Stanford Graduate School of Business.

Sincerely,
Derrick Bolton
Assistant Dean for MBA Admissions

In this letter, Stanford acknowledges that being on the waitlist (or in the "waitpool," in this case) can be frustrating and emphasizes that candidates should not interpret this status negatively ("Please know that you are still a competitive candidate"). Although Stanford does specify a date for an updated decision (March 27, 2013), note that it does not promise a *final* decision at that point. Indeed, the candidate could be accepted into the next class, definitively rejected or even placed on the waitlist again after that initial waiting period. However, the most important part of this letter is this:

> *Please accept a place in the waitpool by submitting the online Waitpool Candidate Reply Form by 6 February 2013. While we are unable to speak individually with you to discuss your candidacy, we hope that the following information will answer your questions and provide you with more details about the waitpool. Thank you for your patience and cooperation in adhering to the waitpool procedure.*

Stanford asks the waitlisted candidate to fill out a simple form and… that is it. The admissions committee cannot, and does not want to, speak with the applicant further about the situation or the individual's qualifications. In Stanford's waitlist FAQs, the school further requests that candidates not attempt any additional correspondence or try to force the admissions committee to interview them:

> *Additional submissions above and beyond the brief letter reaffirming your interest* [the Waitpool Candidate Reply Form]*, are neither requested nor suggested. Interviews are offered on an "invitation only" basis. If you have not had an interview and we feel that one is necessary, we will contact you. Otherwise, please do not travel to Stanford specifically for that purpose. We also are unable to respond to your requests for individual appointments with Stanford Faculty or MBA Admissions Officers.*

Harvard Business School (HBS) also has a closed waitlist policy and is serious about maintaining a level playing field for its candidates still under consideration. In the waitlist FAQs posted on the school's Web site (www.hbs.edu/mba/admissions/waitlist), the admissions committee offers the following guidance:

HBS is fully committed to the online application process. Our decision will be based upon a continued review of the completed application materials you have already submitted. If we need additional information from you as we make a decision on your candidacy we will be in touch, but please refrain from sending in additional materials as they will not be added to your file.

Meanwhile, the Wharton School at the University of Pennsylvania offers similar language on its Web site:

We are unable to offer feedback to candidates while they remain on the list. We are also unable to accept additional materials for inclusion in a waitlisted applicant's file. This policy is designed to create an admissions process that is fair and equitable for all candidates.

Although this should go without saying, when a school's admissions committee stipulates that additional contact is neither necessary nor desired—as Stanford, HBS and Wharton all do in these excerpts—you should follow this directive to the letter. Do not force communication when the admissions committee does not want it.

The only situation in which supplementary input can acceptably be submitted to an admissions committee with a closed waitlist policy is if one of the school's students or a well-placed alumnus/alumna contacts the admissions office on your behalf *but of his or her own volition*. In this case, you would not be violating the school's request, because you would not be doing the contacting yourself. If someone offers to reach out to the admissions committee in support of your candidacy when you are on the waitlist, you must be very clear with this individual that any message sent should not in any way reveal that you have asked for the correspondence to occur. This student or graduate might "put in a good word" via a phone call or email to the admissions office, but this should be the full extent of the contact. Do not try to organize a shadow campaign to bolster your candidacy. A single, well-meaning contact might be helpful, but any more could become annoying—not to mention suspicious—and reflect badly on you.

THE OPEN WAITLIST

Business schools that have an "open" waitlist policy permit—and sometimes even encourage—waitlisted applicants to continue promoting their candidacy by sending a personal update letter or additional relevant information (e.g., new test scores or grades, a promotion). Columbia Business School, the Haas School of Business at the University of California Berkeley and the Ross School of Business at the University of Michigan are a few such schools. The following is a sample waitlist letter from Columbia to a candidate who applied in the school's early decision round:

> *Thank you for applying Early Decision to Columbia Business School. We appreciate your loyalty and commitment. Applicants like you are the core of what is so special about the Columbia community. It is your dedication that makes you unique and Columbia great.*
>
> *After careful review and consideration by the Admissions Committee, we are unable to offer you admission at this time. However, we recognize the strengths of your application and would like to defer our final decision until later in the application cycle. Our intention is to have all early decisions finalized by February 1, 2013, but your final decision may be communicated at any time before then.*
>
> *In order to remain an active candidate for August 2013, please send an email message to [your waitlist manager] with the subject line of "Early Decision - reconsider later." While you are waiting for us to reconsider your application, we encourage you to review your application and determine if there are ways in which it could be strengthened.*
>
> *We frequently get questions regarding this process. We hope the following will answer some of them.*

- When will I receive a final decision?

  We intend to communicate a final decision no later than February 1, 2013, but you may receive a final decision at any time.

- How can I improve my chances of being offered admission?

  We encourage you to review your application and make sure it is your best effort at presenting your personal and professional accomplishments. Please let us know if there has been a change since you submitted your application (improved GMAT score, promotion at work, completion of CFA or other credential or class).

- Can I talk to someone or get feedback from a member of the Admissions Committee?

  Due to the volume of applicants, we cannot accommodate individual requests. A member of the Admissions Committee will contact you if we have specific questions.

  We appreciate your strong interest in Columbia Business School, and we ask for patience and understanding during this process.

Berkeley Haas goes even further in its waitlist FAQs and actually recommends areas that applicants might target to make "substantive, meaningful improvements" in their candidacy:

Below are general suggestions of common areas to address to help enhance your candidacy; not every suggestion will be relevant to each candidate. Focus on substantive, meaningful improvements that you feel will make you a stronger candidate or provide information not already presented in your application. Please note that the Admissions Committee is not able to provide individual feedback regarding the specific area(s) to address while you are on the waitlist. See below for details regarding our feedback policy.

1) Interview – We strongly encourage you to schedule an interview if you have not already had one as a part of the admissions process. Each candidate may only interview once during a given application cycle. Please see below for instructions on how to request an interview.

2) Test scores – If your GMAT or TOEFL scores fall below our averages, you may wish to retake the test and forward an unofficial score (followed by your official score) to the admissions office.

3) Quantitative ability – If you feel you have not sufficiently demonstrated quantitative ability through your undergraduate and graduate level coursework and/or your quantitative subscore on the GMAT, you may wish to enroll in a statistics or calculus course at a local college, retake the GMAT, or do both.

4) Letters of recommendation – You may provide an additional letter of recommendation (or two) to your file, if the letter(s) will add information that was not provided in the original letters submitted.

5) Personal statement – You may submit a new statement to update the Admissions Committee on any significant changes in your professional or personal life since your application was submitted that will add value to your candidacy. Relevant updates may include a promotion, change in employment, updated test score, enrollment or completion of a quantitative course, etc. You may also submit a personal statement if you wish to clarify your career goals or, particularly for those intending to switch careers, provide further detail on steps you have taken to prepare for your career transition.

When you are dealing with an open waitlist, you can rejoice in feeling that you can still influence the committee positively by communicating professional/personal progress since you applied. We do want to caution you, however, that if you decide to send additional information, you must be thoughtful and sparing and take care to strictly follow the admissions committee's guidelines. Before providing any updates, ask yourself, "Is this information I would want to receive if I were evaluating a candidate, or is this just correspondence for its own sake?" We recommend that you limit your interactions and make every one count. In other words, do not flood the admissions committee with additional information. Your target school may be open to receiving supplementary materials, but it is not seeking a constant flow. Persistent emails, multiple additional letters of support and expressions of anxiety on your part about the process are all negatives. Indeed—and we cannot emphasize this enough—resist any temptation to call the school and ask about your status. Such a call will only identify you as a nuisance!

WRITING YOUR WAITLIST LETTER

Now that you have been given the green light to send your target school additional information, you may naturally begin to worry, "What can I offer the admissions committee as an update when I just submitted my application a few months ago?!"

Updating with Quantitative Evidence

Take a moment to pause and reflect on your GMAT scores and your academic transcript: do you feel they accurately represent your quantitative and analytical abilities? If you do not feel confident that they do or you have a weakness in these areas—such as a poor grade in calculus in college or a 65th percentile on the Quantitative section of the GMAT—now would be a good time to address or mitigate this shortcoming. For example, retaking the GMAT or enrolling in a supplemental math class could help you prove to the admissions committee that you truly possess any skills that may be in doubt. Please note, however, that we are not suggesting that you rush to retake the GMAT as a kind of "knee-jerk" reaction, but if you feel that you have room to improve and will likely better your score should you take the exam again, then you should consider doing so. Earning and submitting an improved GMAT score while on the waitlist could help you, but it is not the "ticket" to a guaranteed acceptance—just one piece of the puzzle.

Further, if you have concrete news regarding a promotion in your professional life or if you have assumed additional responsibilities in your community, you should definitely update the MBA admissions committee on this. A promotion is a quantifiable event and can really only be interpreted one way—positively. Likewise, taking a leadership position by directing a community project or joining the board of an organization highlights your commitment and initiative.

Another option is sending an additional recommendation letter that provides a new window into your candidacy. If you have such an option— possibly from a community engagement, side entrepreneurial endeavor or relationship with a mentor—you should submit one new letter (two at the most). However, do not send a letter that offers no new insight into your experience, personality or abilities just to feel that you are providing supplemental information. Exercise judgment and ask yourself, "Can someone out there say something interesting and different about me— something fresh?" If you originally submitted two work recommendations and another supervisor at your company is willing to write a letter on your behalf, that additional recommendation will probably not do anything to advance your candidacy.

Updating with Qualitative Evidence

Many candidates are dismissive of updating the committee with qualitative information, but such data can be quite useful in painting a picture of your ongoing growth. If you have continued networking with the school's students or alumni or have completed a class visit since submitting your application, you can offer a new window into your ever-increasing interest in the school. (When you are on an MBA program's waitlist, the admissions committee wants to know that you are truly committed to the school. Schools want to be certain the candidates they admit are excited and ready to join their program before extending an offer.) Further, even if you have not been promoted, you can creatively reflect on a project that you have started since the application deadline and identify the new professional skills/exposure that this project has provided, such as managing people off-site for the first time or executing certain responsibilities with greater independence. Finally, the personal realm is usually not "off limits," so you should also feel free to discuss any non-work-related accomplishments, such as advancing in your study of a language, visiting a new country or completing a triathlon. By taking a patient, measured approach and thinking creatively when you have been waitlisted, you should be able to provide the admissions committee with powerful supporting materials to bolster your candidacy. Showing your continued professional and personal growth and expressing your sincere and unwavering interest in the school should increase your chances of ultimately gaining admission.

On the following pages, we offer examples of two emails a waitlisted candidate might send her target MBA program.

Sample Letter A: Open Waitlist

Dear Mr. Smith,[1]

Since receiving my waitlist decision one month ago, I have determinedly continued to learn more about the ABC School to be best prepared to join the class, should the opportunity arise. Last week, I visited campus, eager to experience a case discussion firsthand. I admittedly did not expect the manic energy and humor that Professor Paul Johnson brought to the "Finance II" class, but amid his sprints to the board and rapid-fire questioning of the unsuspecting, I learned a profound lesson on the connection between inventory management and working capital needs. I was sold on the case method before my visit, but my experience with the Clarkson Lumber case only reinforced that this is the ideal active learning style for me.[2] I should add

---

1 This is the name of the waitlist manager assigned to the waitlisted student.
2 By including details about her school visit, the candidate shows commitment to and fit with the target program. This text offers some new information about the candidate's current job, though it is not revolutionary.

that I was fortunate to join the learning team of my former colleague Mary Flanagan (a fellow McKinsey alumna) that evening and observed the team dissect the next day's cases. Seeing her engaged in such a collaborative learning environment made me certain that I would be a solid fit both academically and socially.

When I submitted my application, I was about to begin a new case at McKinsey. Today, three months later, this project is quickly moving forward. At McKinsey, I previously worked exclusively on due diligence assessments for private equity firms; I recently asked to join a strategic review and am now evaluating potential divestitures for a media firm.

As I study this firm, I find that I am fascinated by the mix of old media and new media assets and by the nebulous nature of making decisions on assets whose prices seem to change each day. I have repeatedly met with the firm's CFO and its vice president for strategic planning, and we have now determined which assets are "non-core" and are considering options, including selling such expendable assets to competitors or to one of the private equity firms for which I completed a due diligence project. In fact, I was quite proud to have made an introduction for my client to a private equity firm myself.[3] This new experience has been invigorating and has only reinforced my desire to return to McKinsey after completing my MBA, as discussed in depth in my personal statement.[4]

Despite my busy schedule, I remain committed to the Golden Heights Senior Center, where I lead Bingo each Sunday and play in the "house band" each Wednesday night. Last month, I also organized a weekend trip for 20 seniors to the Super Casino and arranged to

---

3 Although she has not received a promotion, she has been enjoying a new experience and new responsibilities at work, and her description provides a sense of her subsequent growth.

4 The applicant confirms her career goals here and reminds the school about her plans to rejoin McKinsey after graduating.

play Bingo there and attend an instrumental show with an acoustic Beatles tribute band.[5] Needless to write, perhaps, it was an experience that none of us will forget.

I remain committed to attending the ABC School next year[6] and am optimistic that I will find a place in your class. I will continue to apprise the admissions committee of my progress and remain available should you have any questions at all.

Sincerely,
Lindsay Garfinkle

Sample Letter B: Open Waitlist

Dear Mr. Smith,

Following up on my update of March 1, 2010, I am writing briefly to notify the admissions committee of two material changes in my candidacy. First, two weeks ago, I completed my "Calculus I" and "Statistics I" classes at the HIJ University Extension School, and yesterday morning, my professors informed me that I earned As in both of their classes. Even though I work in a highly analytical capacity at McKinsey, as a liberal arts major, I felt it important to clearly establish my quantitative competencies, and I am hoping that my As in these recent courses will do so. As soon as my final grades and transcript are available, I will send official copies for your records.[7]

Second, I am excited to report that I took the GMAT for a second time and earned a slightly higher score, a 710. What is noteworthy is that my Quantitative score rose from a 79th percentile to an 85th

---

5   Here the candidate reminds the reader of her outside interests and reinforces her sense of humor, humility, dedication and entrepreneurial spirit.

6   The candidate reiterates her interest in the school.

7   The applicant informs the committee of a very clear and material change in her candidacy and reiterates that she is working to mitigate her potential perceived weakness related to her liberal arts background.

percentile—which I believe serves as further proof of my quant skills and my ability to make contributions in this area. Again, I will follow up shortly by sending my official GMAT score report.[8]

Moreover, I have continued my networking and recently had lunch with David Clarke, ABC MBA '67, who is a partner at McKinsey. I was impressed that all these years later, Mr. Clarke is still active with the alumni association and in touch with, by his estimation, no less than 30 members of his class of 240. In addition to my belief in the case study method, I feel that working closely with my peers and developing enduring relationships is very important.[9] I saw this on display when I visited a class and a learning team meeting with Mary Flanagan last month, and Mr. Clarke's enthusiasm for the school and anecdotes about his class only reinforced my feeling that ABC School is the ideal place for me to live and learn for two years and one I will continue to "experience" throughout my life.

I remain entirely committed to being a member of the ABC School class next year.

Sincerely,
Lindsay Garfinkle

---

8 Again, the writer informs the committee of a material change in her candidacy and reinforces that she has the quantitative skills necessary to succeed in the program.

9 A subtle expression of interest—the candidate is clearly still doing her homework, and the admissions committee can thus be assured that she continues to be interested in this MBA program.

CLOSING THOUGHTS

CLOSING THOUGHTS

Over the years, I have personally conducted thousands of free one-on-one consultations and have spoken before thousands of others through the live in-person and online events that we host in different cities each month (http://www.mbamission.com/blog/category/mbamission-events/). At the end of these sessions and events, the most common question MBA candidates ask me is a version of the following:

"What is the one secret that will get me into my target school?"

Before I respond to this question, allow me to a brief digression. I have been in the admissions consulting business for more than ten years, and I have met with admissions officers from virtually all of the top schools. Each time I encounter one, I say, "I tell candidates all the time that admissions is an art, not a science. I feel silly asking you this, but I want to be sure that I am telling these candidates the truth. Is there a formula for getting into your school?"

My question is always met with a chuckle. I can tell you unequivocally —directly from many admissions officers— that the MBA admissions process is not a code that you need to "crack" and that attempts to game the process or become something that you are not are futile. We offer the words of Stanford GSB's assistant dean and director of MBA admissions, Derrick Bolton, who could not have said it better via his admissions office's Web page:

> *"Because we want to discover who you are, resist the urge to 'package' yourself in order to come across in a way you think Stanford wants. Such attempts simply blur our understanding of who you are and what you can accomplish. We want to hear your genuine voice throughout the essays that you write and this is the time to think carefully about your values, your passions, your hopes and dreams."*

Throughout this book, we have attempted to give you the tools, but certainly not a formula, to create a standout application and grab the admissions committees' attention. Our approach is all about harnessing the inherent power of your personal story. We encourage you to exhaust yourself through multidimensional brainstorming, writing a clear narrative in your voice, creating a resume that reveals consistent accomplishments and other key steps. By doing so, you are not guaranteed to be accepted, but you will tell your best story, and *that* will give you your best shot at being admitted to your target school. And that is what mbaMission is all about...

Sincerely,
Jeremy Shinewald

Do you know that your career won't just advance on its own?
If you want to get ahead, you need

Active Career Management.

No matter where you are in your career, you need to:

Explore Your Values

Look closely at your experiences and what truly matters to you to chart your course at each career step.

Build Relationships

Network effectively to create new opportunities and earn important invitations.

Target Opportunities

Network

Be a Top Performer

Interview

Assess Performance and Chart Growth

Leverage what you already do well and grow where you need to improve.

Talk About Yourself

Promote accomplishments and discuss failures with power, inspiration, and humility.

MBA
Career
Coaches

www.mbacareercoaches.com

Wherever you are in your career, an MBA Career Coach can help you achieve your ambitions through tailored structure, training, and thought partnership as you actively manage your career.

To learn more, sign up for a free consultation today.